PROGRESS & HARD FEELINGS

'Every dramatist stakes out his own territory; and for Doug Lucie it seems to be the brutal and callous power-games that bubble under the surface of modern communal living . . . **Hard Feelings** tore into style-crazed Oxford graduates. And now **Progress** (less venomous but just as funny) exposes the hard underbelly of a slightly older generation of trendy lefties and sexual liberationists living appalling lives in NW6 . . . a brutally satiric eye for modern manners and speech.'
Michael Billington

Hard Feelings
'His setting is a house in Brixton in April 1981. Venetian blinds seal off this privileged barricade from the street riots outside and enable the inmates to get on with their middle-class games . . . But Doug Lucie . . . is doing something more than pin down the lifestyle of London's new swingers. He is suggesting in this pugnacious and funny play that there is a whole generation around that puts style before content, fashion before feeling, and show before basic human sympathy. . . . a genuine dramatist alert to the poignancy of human waste.' *Guardian*

'Mr Lucie's only weapon . . . is that of language, and he uses it with the economy, confidence and wit of a dramatist of twice his age and experience . . . a writer to watch for.' *Sheridan Morley*

'A marvellous social comedy that will make you twitch and wriggle with discomfort at every horrible moment of recognition.' *Time Out*

Progress
'A modish household comprising Will, a Channel 4 researcher, and his wife Ronee, where breakfast is accompanied not by the radio but by the taped sob-outs from his men's therapy group, plus the occasional phone call from Ronee's German girlfriend. The scene is set for a vicious satirical comedy, as appallingly funny as anything Mr Lucie has written . . . Mr Lucie's observation is as gruesomely accurate as ever . . . a masterpiece of comedy.' *Times*

'a brilliantly brutal and funny account of life among the caring classes.' *Observer*.

'A devastatingly nasty farce about a commune of hypocritical "trendy lefties" of the "Big Chill" generation.' *New York Times*

Progress was a smash hit at the Bush Theatre, London, in summer 1984. **Hard Feelings** was also seen at the Bush, and was subsequently shown on telelvision.

D1371999

PROGRESS
&
HARD FEELINGS

DOUG LUCIE

METHUEN · LONDON AND NEW YORK

A METHUEN PAPERBACK

First published in Great Britain as a Methuen Paperback original in 1985 by
Methuen London Ltd, 11 New Fetter Lane, London EC4P 4EE and
in the United States of America by Methuen Inc, 733 Third Avenue, New York, NY 10017.
Copyright © 1985 by Doug Lucie

Lucie, Doug
    Progress; &, Hard feelings.
    I. Title   II. Lucie, Doug. Hard feelings
    822'.914   PR6062.U1/

    ISBN 0-413-57760-0

Printed in Great Britain by Expression Printers Ltd, London N7.

CAUTION
This play is fully protected by copyright. All enquiries concerning the rights for professional
or amateur stage productions should be addressed to Michael Imison Playwrights Ltd,
28 Almeida Street, London N1. No performance may be given unless a licence has been
obtained.

PROGRESS

Progress was first presented at the Bush Theatre, London on 2 July, 1984, with the following cast:

RONEE, *33 years old. She is an administrator of a*   Lindsay Duncan
South London Community and Arts Centre. A tough,
articulate woman.

WILL, *34 years old. Ronee's husband. He is a Current*   Gregory Floy
Affairs researcher at Channel 4. Very much Ronee's male
equivalent, though he is slightly in awe of her.

OLIVER, *31 years old. A crafts stallholder. He is small*   David Bamber
and very talkative, particularly when drunk.

MARTIN, *29 years old. He is supposedly Oliver's*   Kevin Elyot
bisexual live-in companion. He is witty and superficially
callous.

BRUCE, *32 years old. A barman. He cultivates a*   Struan Rodger
quiet, rather macho image. He is shy, with a stammer.

ANGE, *20 years old. A young wife staying with Ronee*   Sharon Maiden
and Will, having left her husband after he beat her. Shy and
reserved, though with a tough streak.

LENNY, *21 years old. Ange's husband. He is a car*   Perry Fenwick
mechanic, conventionally inarticulate, but with animal
cunning and an evil sense of humour.

MARK, *32 years old. He is Ronee's and Will's tenant, a*   David Cardy
journalist on the Daily Express. *Outspoken, a constant*
stream of fairly tasteless jokes being his trademark. He is
already going to seed, but regards himself as irresistible.

Directed by David Hayman
Designed by Geoff Rose
Lighting by Bart Cossee
Sound by Annie Hutchinson

ACT ONE

Scene One

Tuesday morning, 10 a.m.
RONEE *is at the table eating muesli and fruit for breakfast.* WILL *is standing in his dressing gown, rubbing his hair with a towel. She's leafing through* The Guardian *while on the stereo a tape recording of* OLIVER's *voice plays.*

OLIVER: . . . To see him like that. Terrible, just terrible. (*Beat.*) And he denies it, y'know? He can hardly stand up. And he looks me in the eye and says, 'Ollie, on my mother's grave, I haven't touched a drop'. (WILL *goes off.*) And when I point out that gran was cremated and therefore doesn't have a grave . . . (*Pause.*) And the next thing. 'All right, Ollie, I admit it. I might have had one or two'. One or two. The amount of vodka he gets through, he's single-handedly keeping the Russian economy afloat. And then it's tears. He breaks down. Y'know? Your own father grovelling around on the floor, begging you to forgive him. I mean, Christ, it hurts. (*Pause. The sound of a drink being poured.*) And, like, my kid brother, it cracks him up completely. He drinks himself senseless. It gets the whole family. My mother doesn't speak to any of us, hardly, any more.

RONEE: Clever girl.

OLIVER: And that's the point. It's her I feel most sorry for. Thirty-five years married to the guy, and he turns out a jerk. What can you say? Tough luck, Mum? (*Pause.*) She's in the WI, y'know. She's not exactly a sister, if you know what I mean. (*Pause.*) I hate him for what he's done. But he is my father. (WILL *enters, partly dressed.*) Can anybody give me any idea what I can do?

RONEE: Switch that awful little twerp off, will you?

OLIVER: I need help.

WILL *switches off the tape.*

RONEE: How many hours of tape have you got with that drunk going on about his father?

WILL: It's not always his father. There's also non-aggressive football supporting, coming to terms with a bisexual nature, and the problems of getting your non-patriarchal leg over. (*Beat.*) He does need help though.

RONEE: He needs a psychiatrist, not a mens' group.

WILL: Ronee, love, we're trying.

The phone rings.

RONEE: I'll say. (*She answers the phone.*) Hello. Oh, hi. Wie geht's? (*Beat.*) Ja, richtig. Das werden fabulos sein. (*Beat.*) 'The Poison Girls.' Feminist Gruppe. (*She laughs.*) Liar. Du verstehst. (*Beat.*) OK. Sechs Uhr. Ja. (*She glances in* WILL's *direction. He's leafing through the paper.*) Ich liebe dich. OK. Tschuss. (*She puts the phone down.*)

WILL: My clipping got in 'Naked Ape'.

RONEE: I saw.

WILL: Spelled my name wrong, though.

RONEE: I saw that too.

WILL: How's Andrea?

RONEE: Fine.

WILL: She hasn't been round for ages. I'd love to see her. Why don't you ask her to dinner some time? (*Pause.*) It'd just be nice, that's all I mean.

RONEE: No.

WILL: It's not very fair. She's not your property.

RONEE: I saw her first.

MARK *enters. He looks as if he's been up for hours, though he hasn't.*

MARK: Yo. (*He goes straight to* RONEE *and points at her nipples, which are showing under her t-shirt.*) Is it cold in here, or are you just glad to see me?

She starts to go.

That was fantastic last night. Best ever. Don't let on to Will, though. Don't want to make him jealous.

She's gone.

Morning, brother.

WILL: Good morning, Mark. I'm trying to read the paper, so shut up.

MARK: That rag? Call that a paper? This is a paper. (*He holds up* The Express.) And I should know. (*He opens it up.*) Oh, yes. I like it. Look at that. (*He spreads the paper out on the table.*) All my own work.

WILL *stares at it.*

WILL: Mark, tell me, what exactly *is* a love nest?

MARK: Depends. In this case it's a council house where a dypso has-been D.J. lives on the dole with a very tasty social worker.

WILL: And you don't think maybe he'd like to be left alone?

MARK: Bollocks. He loved it. He's making a come-back, see?

ANGE *comes in. She's wearing a see-through blouse over which she's about to put on a jumper.* MARK *points at her breasts.*

If you're selling those puppies, I'll have the one on the right with the brown nose.

She quickly puts the jumper on.

Spoilt a lovely view.

WILL: Hi. Make yourself some breakfast if you want.

ANGE: Ta. (*She goes out to the kitchen.*)

MARK: You dirty dog.

WILL: Mark . . .

MARK: I don't suppose she wants to make an old man very happy.

WILL: Her name is Ange. She's staying here for a few days on account of her husband keeps using her for a sparring partner and she doesn't box. She doesn't need you breathing down her neck.

MARK: It's not her neck I want to breathe down.

WILL: Give it a rest.

MARK: Rest? Bloody hell, rest's about right. Last night I picked up this nymphomaniac . . .

WILL: I don't want to hear.

MARK: . . . Went back to her place, I was done in by midnight. And she kept farting non-stop. Had to scrape the duvet off the ceiling. Then this morning, I woke up, I felt so rough I had to have a wank to get

my heart started.

RONEE *appears at the door.*

RONEE: See you.

WILL: What time'll you be back?

RONEE: Late. We've got a social tonight.

WILL: I could drop in . . .

RONEE: Women only.

WILL: Ah.

MARK: A woman's place is in the oven, that's what I always say.

RONEE: If you could be late with the rent just once, so I could kick you out.

MARK: You love it, really.

RONEE: Oh, get cancer.

She goes. He shouts after her.

MARK: Don't forget to leave the window open. I'll be up that drainpipe. (*A door slams.*) Here, this fella's walking down the street, sees an old mate. He thinks, funny, he looks like a woman. So he says, 'What's happened to you?' Fella says, 'I've done it, I've had the operation.' So this bloke says, 'Didn't it hurt?' Other bloke says, 'No.' He says, 'What, not when they give you tits?' He says, 'No.' He says, 'Not when they, y'know cut it off?' He says, 'No.' Then he says, 'I'll tell you what did hurt, that's when they shrunk my brain and widened my mouth.' (*He laughs.*)

WILL: Jesus. You should see someone, y'know. Get professional help.

MARK: I've got it. Swedish massage in Brewer Street.

ANGE *comes in with a bowl of cereal.*

Hello again.

ANGE: 'Lo.

MARK: I'm Mark. I live in the attic.

ANGE: Oh.

MARK: If you ever feel like coming up to see my etchings . . .

ANGE: Don't think so.

MARK: The door's always open.

WILL: Have a bit of tact, will you?

MARK: Most tactful man in Fleet Street, me.

WILL: This isn't Fleet Street.

MARK: Don't you believe it. We get everywhere. (*Beat.*) Talking of which, I'd better get to work. I'm after some woofter pop singer today.

WILL: God . . .

MARK: Horrible little fudge-packer.

WILL: Just go, will you?

MARK: I'm on my bike. (*To* ANGE *as he goes*:) Hey, don't forget to leave your window open tonight. I'll be straight up that drainpipe.

WILL: D'you know what time you'll be back?

MARK: No idea. Tell you what, if I'm not in bed by twelve, I'll come home.

WILL: Don't come barging in if I've got people here.

MARK: You should let me in. I'm great fun at orgies.

He goes.

WILL: That was supposed to be a joke.

ANGE: Eh?

WILL: Orgies. You look worried. (*Pause.*) Sit down, make yourself at home. (*She does.*) He's all mouth and trousers.

ANGE: He's creepy.

WILL: Sitting tenant, I'm afraid. Comes with the house. Our resident damp patch. (*Pause.*) Hey look, while you're here, treat the place like your own. Don't feel . . Inhibited or anything. (*She nods.*) It's rough for you, I know. Anything we can do, just say.

ANGE: Ta. (*Pause.*) Cup of tea? I made a pot.

WILL: Yeah, lovely.

She gets up and goes to the kitchen. He stares at her and takes a deep breath and raises his eyebrows, or does something to indicate he finds her attractive. He goes over to the stereo and turns on the tape quietly. We can't make out what's being said. ANGE *comes back in with two cups of tea. He takes his tea and sips.*

Great. Worker's tea. Ronee always makes the perfumed stuff. Earl Grey. Me, I'm an unashamed PG Tips man.

(*Pause.*) What I call worker's tea. (*He switches off the tape.*)

ANGE: What's that?

WILL: It's a tape of the men's group that meets round here. (*She looks blank.*) We talk about things . . . Try to understand and come to terms with sexism, relationships, that kind of stuff. We're trying to change our attitudes by being open and supportive without resorting to traditional, hierarchical structures. (*Beat.*) Trying to prove that not all men are monsters.

ANGE: Oh.

WILL: Y'know, like your husband.

Pause.

ANGE: He's just a rotten git.

WILL: Yeah, well . . . (*Pause.*) I can never understand a man hitting a woman. I don't mean that in a sexist way, chivalry, all that crap. I mean, it seems such a pointless thing to do. So negative.

ANGE: Well, I did hit him with the frying pan.

Pause.

WILL: Why?

ANGE: Tried to put my head through the window, didn't he?

WILL: When it was shut?

ANGE: 'Course.

WILL: Not very nice.

ANGE: No. He's a rotten git.

WILL: Then he hit you, did he?

ANGE: Yeah.

WILL: Poor kid. (*Pause.*) This is great tea. You can come again. (*Pause.*) Well, I better stroll into work, I suppose. (*He puts on his socks, shoes and jacket.*) D'you work?

ANGE: Only down the Centre.

WILL: Right. Ronee told me.

ANGE: Lenny don't like the idea of me going to work.

WILL: Bit prehistoric, your Lenny. Drags you around by the hair as well, does he? (*She shrugs.*) Maybe he should join our group.

ANGE: He's got his mates. He goes out on the piss with them. Right rotten lot, they are. Do some rotten things. (*Pause.*) D'you know what they done? Last year?

WILL: Shock me.

ANGE: They went camping down Cornwall. Before we was married, this is. And they was at this disco, and they got Bobby – he's the nice one, that's why they call him Bobby, out of Dallas – and they stripped him naked, nude, y'know, and they handcuffed him to this girl in the disco. And Bobby and this girl had to go all the way back to the campsite to get the key. And they wouldn't let her go. They never done nothing to her, but they kept her there. And they all thought it was dead funny. Then her boyfriend came and got her, but he couldn't do nothing 'cause there's like eight of them. I mean, and they thought it was dead funny.

WILL: Sad, very sad. (*He's dressed: t-shirt, jeans, kickers.*) Right. Well, look, I'll see you tonight. Help yourself to food and anything else. Ronee gave you a key, did she?

ANGE: Yeah.

WILL: OK. I'll see you later. Take care.

He goes. She looks round the room, ending up at the stereo. She turns on the tape, picks up the two cups and goes to the kitchen as WILL's *voice plays on the tape:*

Basically, what we're talking about, I suppose, is understanding our own maleness.

Fade.

Scene Two

Monday lunchtime.
   ANGE *comes into the room with a sandwich and a cup of tea. Radio One is playing on the stereo. She sits on the sofa and flips through a copy of* Spare Rib. *The doorbell rings. She looks up. It rings again. She gets up and goes through to the front door. Pause.* LENNY *appears.* ANGE *follows him in, and turns off the radio.*

ANGE: I never said you could come in.

LENNY: I'm in now, ain't I?

ANGE: This ain't your house.

LENNY: Ain't yours, neither. (*Pause.*) Bit tasty, this, innit?

ANGE: What you want?

LENNY: Come to look at the drains, ain't I? What the fuck d' you think I want?

ANGE: Don't start swearing.

Pause.

LENNY: Don't I get a cup of tea?

ANGE: No. (*Pause.*) How'd you know I was here?

LENNY: I asked down the Centre. (*Pause. He takes a piece of paper out of his pocket and gives it to her.*) Here.

ANGE: What is it?

LENNY: Open it up. Find out.

She does.

ANGE: Oh, God . . .

LENNY: Read it, then.

ANGE: Don't want to.

LENNY: Why not?

ANGE: 'Cause I don't.

Pause.

LENNY: I wrote it for you.

ANGE: I didn't think you wrote it for the milkman.

LENNY: Read it.

ANGE: I've read your poems before.

LENNY: It's a different one though, innit? It's a new one. Go on.

She gives it a cursory reading.

ANGE: Yeah. Lovely.

LENNY: You never read it.

ANGE: I did.

LENNY: You never. Takes longer than that. Read it properly.

ANGE: I have read it properly.

Pause.

LENNY: Rotten cow.

Pause. She reads it again.

ANGE: There.

LENNY: Like it?

ANGE: Dunno.

LENNY: What d'you mean? Dunno?

ANGE: I mean, I dunno.

LENNY: Don't be stupid. Either you like it or you don't.

ANGE: I like it.

LENNY: Good. (*Pause.*) How come I don't get a cup of tea?

ANGE: 'Cause you ain't staying.

LENNY: Says who?

ANGE: I do.

He takes a packet of sandwiches out of his overalls pocket.

LENNY: I've got to have something to wash me dinner down.

ANGE: What d'you think you're doing?

LENNY: It's me dinner. This is me dinner hour so I'm gonna have me dinner.

ANGE: Not here you ain't.

He stuffs a sandwich in his mouth.

LENNY: Bleedin' well am.

ANGE: You horrible pig. (*Beat.*) Who made them, then?

LENNY: Me mum. (*Beat.*) Egg and cress. Lovely.

ANGE: You don't like egg.

LENNY: I do the way me mum does it.

ANGE: You can't do nothing with egg, 'cept boil it.

LENNY: She mashes it up. With salad cream. Tasty.

ANGE: Get food poisoning if your mum made it.

LENNY: Dead tasty.

He eats. She goes to the kitchen. He looks round the room. He picks up the Spare Rib *and reads it. She comes back in with a cup of tea.*

What the fucking hell d'you call this?

She snatches it off him.

ANGE: I call it a magazine. What d'you call it?

LENNY: Pile o' crap, I call it.

ANGE: It's nothing to do with you.

LENNY: Load o' bollocks. (*Pause.*) Here, Dink and Wobbler had a scrap last night. Down the Duke. Dink bust his finger. (*Beat.*) Pretty good scrap, they reckon.

Pause.

ANGE: Kids.

LENNY: Eh?

ANGE: Nothing.

LENNY: What?!

ANGE: Kids! You are. Bloody scraps. Bloody stupid nicknames. You're supposed to grow outa that sorta thing when you leave school, y'know.

Pause.

LENNY: They're *my* mates.

ANGE: You can have them.

Pause.

LENNY: Right. When you coming back?

ANGE: You what?

LENNY: I got the motor outside. You can dump your gear in it now if you like. Don't matter if I'm a bit late back. (*Pause.*) You ain't making a lot of noise here, doll. (*Pause.*) C'mon. You've usually got enough rabbit for both of us.

ANGE: 'S not true. I can't say nothing, case you don't like it.

LENNY: Only when you're talking crap.

ANGE: Yeah. Which is most of the time, according to you.

LENNY: Well, you ain't exactly Mastermind, are you?

ANGE: Which university did you go to, then?

Beat.

LENNY: I asked you a question. When you coming back?

ANGE: Dunno.

LENNY: Don't know fuck all, you. (*Pause.*) Listen, I ain't got time to muck about. Get your stuff. (*Beat.*) C'mon.

ANGE: I ain't going nowhere. Not yet.

Beat.

LENNY: Ange. 'Case you've forgotten, you're my wife.

ANGE: 'Case you've forgotten, I ain't a punch-bag.

LENNY: You're my wife.

ANGE: Makes it all right, does it?

LENNY: You ain't s'posed to piss off every time we have a bit of a barney.

ANGE: What *am* I s'posed to do?

Beat.

LENNY: What other women do.

ANGE: What, like Rose?

LENNY: Like Rose what?

ANGE: Your rotten brother breaks her nose and won't even let her go to the hospital, 'case the Old Bill do him for it. I ain't standing for nothing like that.

LENNY: When'd I ever break your nose?

ANGE: Had a bloody good try.

LENNY: 'S just a little tap. Anyway, you hit me.

ANGE: You hit me first.

Pause.

LENNY: Look . . . I won't. All right? I won't hit you again.

ANGE: Pigs might fly.

LENNY: I won't. (*Beat.*) I never knew you was gonna leave, did I? Wouldn't have hit you if I did.

ANGE: What do you expect me to do? (*Pause.*) Eh?

LENNY: I dunno. (*Pause.*) Me mum never left me dad when he hit her.

ANGE: I ain't your mum. And I ain't gonna end up like her, neither.

LENNY: What you mean?

ANGE: You know what I mean. You can end up like your dad if you want, but I ain't ending up like your mum.

LENNY: I dunno what you're on about.

ANGE: Don't you?

LENNY: No.

Beat.

ANGE: Comin' home from work, and if your dinner ain't on the table shouting your head off and kicking the poor bloody dog's what I'm on about. Not letting my mates in the house is what I'm on about. And if they do manage to get past the front bloody door, telling us to shut up 'cause you're watching 'Crossroads' is what I'm bloody on about.

LENNY: Well, you sat there jabbering on. Drives me fucking mad.

ANGE: And you sat there, like bloody God in front of the bloody telly. Drives me mad.

LENNY: What's wrong with watching the telly all of a sudden? I work bloody hard all day, I wanna come home and relax.

ANGE: With your flies undone.

LENNY: You what?

ANGE: You always undo your trousers, soon as you get in that chair.

Beat.

LENNY: What's that got to do with anything?

ANGE: I hate it.

LENNY: What? Me undoing me trousers?

ANGE: Yeah. It's gross. (*He looks puzzled.*) D'you now what I'm talking about?

LENNY: I ain't got a fucking clue.

ANGE: That's it, innit? You ain't. You don't understand nothing I say 'cause you never listen. (*The door slams.*) Oh, Christ, now I'm for it.

MARK (*from the hallway*): Lock up your daughters, 'cause . . . (*He enters and sees* LENNY. *Pause.*) How do.

LENNY: Wotcher.

Pause.

ANGE: 'S Lenny. My husband.

MARK: Oh, right. Pleased to meet you. (*They shake.*) Thought perhaps you were a burglar. (*Feeble laugh.*) Mark. I live in the attic. (*Beat.*) Uh . . . I forgot my address book. Had to pop back and get it. (*Beat.*) Upstairs.

He goes.

LENNY: Who's that then?

ANGE: I dunno. I just met him this morning. He's a creep.

LENNY: Yeah? Looked a bit glad to see you, didn't he?

ANGE: How should I know?

Pause.

LENNY: Where you kipping, then?

ANGE: You what? Upstairs.

LENNY: Yeah, in the attic?

ANGE: Bloody hell. You're cracked you are. I only met him this morning.

LENNY: So what's he doing here now?

ANGE: He lives here, for God's sake. And he said, 'forgot his address book,' didn't he?

LENNY: What, you think I just stepped off the banana boat?

ANGE: Wish you'd step off a bloody cliff.

LENNY (*standing*): Ange . . .

MARK *reappears.*

MARK: Here we are, then. (*He holds up his address book.*)

LENNY: Do us another cup of tea, will you?

ANGE *goes to the kitchen.*

MARK: That's OK. I haven't got time. (*He puts the box in his case.*) You patching things up?

LENNY: What's it to you?

MARK: Me? Sod all. (*Pause.*) None of my business, pal. I just live here. Tenant, that's all I am. I don't have any say in who comes in and out. That's all down to Will and Ronee. Well, Ronee.

LENNY: She the bint from the Centre?

MARK: Yeah. Miss Bra Burner of sixty-eight. Mind you, he's no better. Can't say a bloody word round here without getting your head bitten off. Trendy lefties. About as much fun as a plane crash.

LENNY: You can always move.

MARK: Do us a favour. NW6, highly des. res.? Twenty-five quid a week? I wouldn't move if we had Brezhnev in the basement. Which, for all I know, we might very well have. (ANGE *comes back in and gives* LENNY *his tea.*) Anyway, I've got to go stake out some woofter pop singer. (*They look confused.*) I'm a journalist.

LENNY: Yeah?

MARK: God's gift to the gutter press. Don't you believe it. So, I'll see you.

LENNY: See you.

MARK *goes.*

Journalist, is he?

ANGE: That's what he said.

Beat.

LENNY: This tea's rotten.

ANGE: Hard luck.

LENNY: Trying to poison me, are you?

ANGE: If you don't want it . . . (*She goes to take it.*)

LENNY: Leave off . . .

ANGE: If it's so bloody rotten . . . (*He snatches it back from her and spills some.*) Oh, you pig. (*She rushes out. He smiles and slowly starts to pour more on the floor. She comes back with a cloth.*) What you doing?

LENNY: It's good for the shag pile.

ANGE: You bloody pig. (*She goes down on all fours and rubs the carpet.*)

LENNY (*laughing*): Fucking look at you.

ANGE: What's funny?

LENNY: Mrs Fucking Mop. Got you skivvying for them, have they? Doing the dishes?

ANGE: No. Fuck off. (LENNY *laughs again. Pause.*) I'll have to shampoo this . . .

He suddenly goes down on his knees behind her and holds her hips tightly. She freezes.

LENNY: You coming home?

Pause.

ANGE: No.

Blackout.

Scene Three

Monday. 7 p.m.
   BRUCE *is sitting in one of the chairs. He is gripping a wrist strengthener. A door slams off stage. RONEE enters and puts her bag on the table.*

RONEE: Hello, Bruce. (*He raises his hand and gives a half-smile.*) Where's Will?

BRUCE: Uh . . . probably, I think . . . In the kitchen, maybe.

RONEE: He's not cooking, is he?

BRUCE: Yeah, well . . . He mentioned . . . something, uh, Chinese.

RONEE: Delia Smith, eat your heart out.

BRUCE: Spare . . . ribs in, uh, black bean sauce. I think.

RONEE: Sounds ridiculous enough.

She goes out and upstairs.

BRUCE: Uh, yeah.

He starts clenching again. WILL *enters.*

WILL: Did I hear Ronee?

BRUCE: Yeah.

   WILL *goes to the door and shouts upstairs.*

WILL: Ronee?

RONEE (*off*): What?

WILL: What are you doing?

RONEE (*off*): Getting changed.

WILL: Oh, right. D'you want some food?

RONEE: I've eaten.

WILL: Ribs in black bean sauce.

RONEE (*off*): I've eaten.

WILL: OK. Sometimes I think my wife doesn't like my cooking. Help yourself to a drink, Bruce.

He goes. BRUCE *goes to the drinks. He pours a vodka, holds the glass up and downs it in one. He puts the glass down and takes a can of beer. As he sits and opens it,* RONEE *enters, changed, and gets her bag. As she goes she calls to* WILL *in the kitchen:*

RONEE: Don't wait up for me.

She goes.

WILL (*off*): What? (*He appears.*) What?

BRUCE: Don't wait . . . up for me. She said.

WILL: Jesus, she could have waited.

Pause.

BRUCE: Uh . . . Maybe she . . . needs space . . .

WILL (*pouring a glass of wine*): Ollie and Martin are late.

BRUCE (*looking at his watch*): Six . . . minutes.

WILL: Yeah. (*Pause. They are not very comfortable together.*) You had any joy with the flat-hunting?

BRUCE: I saw a . . . flat at the, uh, Oval?

WILL: Any good?

BRUCE: Great.

WILL: Problem settled, then.

BRUCE: Uh, no.

WILL: How come?

BRUCE: Like . . . Uh, it's got three . . . skinheads squatting in it.

WILL: Ah. Slight problem.

BRUCE: Right.

Pause.

WILL: Is it council?

BRUCE: Yeah.

WILL: They'll evict them, won't they?

BRUCE: Well . . . Yeah, but . . . Really heavy . . . Police and everything . . . Lot of hassle . . .

WILL: I suppose it would be.

BRUCE: So, uh . . . I guess something'll . . . Come up.

WILL: Best of luck.

BRUCE (*taking some small bottles out of his bag*): Want some . . . Vitamins?

WILL: No. Thanks. (BRUCE *takes some.*) Eat healthy food, you don't need them.

BRUCE: They're just, y'know . . . A boost.

WILL: Sure.

BRUCE: And . . . I don't enjoy it, uh, cooking, a lot . .

WILL: I love it, I really do. It's a hobby for me and it liberates Ronee.

BRUCE: Sort of . . . reversal of, uh, roles . . .

WILL: Yeah, sort of. (*Beat.*) And it's so bloody easy, y'know. Take this thing I'm knocking up now. When I first read the recipe, I thought, Jesus, stroll on, back to the drawing board. But then I made it a couple of times and now, I can do it from memory. Chop the garlic, ginger, onion, soak the black beans, mix it all together with sherry, soya sauce and water, fry the ribs for five minutes, drain off the oil, put in the black bean mixture, stir fry for half a minute, cover and heat for ten minues, put in cornflour, water and sugar, stir fry very hot, hey presto. No sweet and sour and a number ninety-three to go, please. This is the genuine article.

Pause.

BRUCE: I, uh . . . can't . . . wait . . .

WILL: You'll have to, till Ollie and Martin get here, I'm afraid. Help yourself to drink.

He starts to go.

BRUCE: I'm OK . . . Thanks.

Pause. WILL goes. BRUCE goes to the drinks and pours another vodka and downs it in one. The doorbell rings.

WILL (*off*): Get that, will you, Bruce?

BRUCE *goes to the door. As soon as he opens it, we can hear* OLIVER *talking, very fast, very agitated.*

OLIVER: Hi, Bruce. Sorry I'm late. Fucking Martin. (*They enter.*) He's not here by the remotest bloody chance, is he? No. 'Course he isn't. Where is he? Your guess is as good as mine, mate. That man is a walking bloody disaster area. I haven't seen any trace of him since last night. Lunch today? No show. Help me out on the stall this afternoon so I can go and see the bank manager? No bloody show. Meet at six in the Dragon? Ha. And where is he? Check missing persons. It's your best bet. I need a drink. (*He pours a huge glass of red wine.*) He could be lying headless in the Thames mud for all I know. I mean, I need this, y'know? I really need this.

WILL *enters.*

Will, I'm sorry. Fucking Martin. I'd've been here hours ago, except he didn't show up. I've been hanging on.

WILL: No bother.

OLIVER: What does he think he's up to? Ask him. If he ever turns up. You ask him. 'Cause he won't tell me. Might as well talk to the trees for all the information I get out of fucking Martin.

WILL: Calm down, mate. We've got all night.

OLIVER: But it's not fair, though, is it? I mean it's not fair to me, it's not fair to you. I'm really going to give him a piece of my mind this time. He's completely buggered up my day. (*Beat.*) I know it's negative but I am bloody furious.

Pause.

BRUCE: Would you . . . like some vitamins?

OLIVER: Peace of mind, Bruce, that's all I need. A little bit of mental tranquility is what I'm after.

WILL *pours another glass of wine.*

BRUCE: But apart from that . . . Mrs Lincoln . . . What did you, uh . . .

OLIVER: Think of the play.

BRUCE: Think of . . .

Beat.

OLIVER: It's the way you tell 'em, Bruce.

Slight discomfort.

WILL: No point starting without Martin, is there, really?

OLIVER: Will, I don't know if he's still even in the country, let alone anywhere near the vicinity of North West London. Start if you like.

WILL: Let's give it a few minutes. (*Beat.*) Hey, I might have something quite interesting for us tonight.

BRUCE (*to* OLLIE): Spare ribs . . . in . . .

WILL: No, not the food.

BRUCE: Oh.

WILL: One of the women from the Centre's been staying here. Her husband's been bashing her about. Ronee brought her back last night. You should see her, poor kid.

OLIVER: That makes my blood boil. What sort of man does that?

WILL: Anyway, I thought if she was up to it, we could maybe talk to her.

OLIVER: I don't know . . .

WILL: I don't mean give her the third degree. I mean talk. Constructively. Positively. Y'know, show support.

OLIVER: Probably frighten her to death.

WILL: Well, obviously, if . . .

BRUCE: It's the husband . . . we should . . . talk to.

OLIVER: The thing is, Will, we're supposed to be helping ourselves, right? The group is for us to examine ourselves. (*Beat.*) It's pornography tonight. That's what I've come to talk about. Pornography. I've been working on it all week.

Pause.

WILL: Sure. OK. Pornography it is.

The doorbell rings. WILL goes out. OLLIE pours another drink. Voices outside. WILL and MARTIN enter.

The prodigal returns.

MARTIN: Hi, gang. Sorry I'm late. Will, I could severely molest a G and T, if that's OK.

WILL: Sure. (*He pours it.*)

MARTIN: Didn't start without me, did you?

WILL: No.

MARTIN: Good. (WILL *hands him his drink.*) Thanks. Everybody have a good day?

WILL: So-so.

MARTIN: Bruce? Good day?

BRUCE: I . . . saw a film.

MARTIN: Good film?

BRUCE: Uh . . . No.

Beat.

MARTIN: Ollie? Good day? (*Beat.*) Ollie?

OLIVER: What?

MARTIN: Did you have a good day? (*Silence.*) You do like to keep us

guessing, don't you?

OLIVER: I had a fucking awful day.

Beat.

MARTIN: Uh-huh.

Pause.

WILL: What about you?

MARTIN: Me? Well, one day's very much the same as another, really, I tend to find. They all sort of merge. I'm never quite sure where one ends and another begins. So today was . . . another day. Didn't exactly register on the Richter scale or anything.

OLIVER: God . . .

MARTIN *looks at him. Pause.*

WILL: I've still got a couple of things to do in the kitchen. Won't be a minute. (*As he goes, he touches* BRUCE *on the shoulder.*)

BRUCE: I want to, uh, see . . . how he does it . . . Chinese . . .

He goes.

MARTIN: My God, how bloody polite. (*Pause.*) OK. Let's have it, Ollie.

OLIVER: Martin, you've no idea how disappointed, how let down, I feel.

MARTIN: Don't be daft. Of course I have.

OLIVER: Then how can you . . . ? (*Pause.*) What did you do last night?

MARTIN: Oh, I went to a party.

OLIVER: Whose?

MARTIN: Piers and Molly. You know Piers and . . .

OLIVER: I don't know Piers and Molly.

MARTIN: I'm sure you do.

OLIVER: I do not.

MARTIN: I thought you met them at Sandra's that time . . . (*Pause.*) Maybe not.

OLIVER: No.

MARTIN: I'll invite them round. You'd love Molly, she's a scream.

OLIVER: Where?

MARTIN: Where is she a scream?

OLIVER: Where was the party?

MARTIN: Oh. At Piers and Molly's.

OLIVER: Which is where?

Pause.

MARTIN: Let me get this right. You're asking me these absurd questions because you think what?

OLIVER: Where were you?

MARTIN: Because you think I was . . . What?

OLIVER: Where?

MARTIN: I was what?

OLIVER: Screwing around!

Pause. MARTIN starts to laugh. He gets up and looks round the room.

MARTIN (*opening a cupboard*): No. No one there. (*He looks under the sofa.*) No. The room is empty. Apart from us. (*Beat.*) So. Who's it for? Who are you trying to kid?

OLIVER: You were going to look after the stall this afternoon.

MARTIN (*genuine*): Ah, I forgot. Honest.

OLIVER: Why?

MARTIN: I don't know. (*Beat.*) I'm sorry.

OLIVER: Martin, believe me, you tear me apart sometimes. (*Pause.*) D'you know what I'm sayng?

MARTIN: Yes.

OLIVER: We've both made a commitment. We've both got to keep it up.

MARTIN: I really did forget. (*Pause.*) So, did you get to the bank?

OLIVER: How could I?

Pause.

MARTIN: I'll do the stall all day tomorrow. How's that?

OLIVER: It's something.

MARTIN: Take the day off. Have fun or something.

OLIVER: Yeah.

MARTIN: Look, don't let's fight.

OLIVER: OK.

Pause.

MARTIN: Perhaps I ought to let Will and Bruce know we're . . .

OLIVER: I'll do it. (*He starts to go.*) I need you, mate.

MARTIN: I need you too.

OLLIE *goes.* MARTIN *breathes out loudly and gets another drink as* BRUCE *comes in. They look at each other. Pause.*

All sorted out.

BRUCE *nods. He goes to the drinks, pours a vodka and drinks it down in one.* MARTIN *smiles. They look at each other.* MARTIN *throws a glance at the door and turns back. They kiss.* BRUCE *sits down as* WILL *and* OLLIE *come back in.*

WILL: . . . No, light soya sauce you use more with fish or chicken. In South East Asian food, mainly.

OLIVER: Oh, I see.

WILL: Talking of which, did you get to that Malayan place I told you about?

MARTIN: No, not yet.

WILL: Well, don't forget. You'll thank me.

MARTIN: We could try it tomorrow, couldn't we, Ollie?

OLIVER: Yeah, why not?

They all settle.

WILL: OK. Why don't we get started?

OLIVER: Whose turn is it to chair?

WILL (*setting up the tape recorder*): I did it last week.

OLIVER: So . . . alphabetically . . . It's Bruce's turn.

MARTIN: Will – by the way, how's Ronee?

WILL: Busy. Very busy.

MARTIN: She's an amazing lady.

WILL: I know.

OLIVER: I believe we covered the use of the word 'lady' in our first meeting, didn't we?

MARTIN: Deliberate irony, Ollie.

OLIVER: Sloppy consciousness, Martin. Very sloppy.

MARTIN: I know. 'Chick, bint, skirt, tart,

crumpet, tail, little woman, wifey, bit of stuff'. These words will never again pass my lips.

OLIVER: Or 'lady'.

MARTIN: You really are becoming a little commissar, you know that?

OLIVER: It's important. It's what this is all about. What's the point of changing the way we behave if we don't change the way we speak? Y'know?

MARTIN: Right on.

Beat.

WILL: Tape's running. OK, Bruce.

BRUCE: Right. Uh . . . Pornography. Shall we . . . do it as normal . . . ?

MARTIN: Beg your pardon?

BRUCE: I mean . . . Like we . . . Someone start off and . . . Y'know . . .

OLIVER: I think we should start by talking about our experience of pornography. As men. Be honest about it. OK?

MARTIN: Off you go, Ollie.

Beat.

OLIVER: OK. I've used pornography. In the past. I'm ashamed to say it, but it's true.

WILL: Why are you ashamed to say it?

OLIVER: Because I feel I've exploited fellow human beings. Namely, women. Merely to satisfy selfish male desires. And, I mean, it doesn't stop there does it? Once you've seen one picture of a woman offering herself to you, that's it. The mind automatically makes the connection: all women are like that. Because it appeals to immaturity. We've all got that bit of us that's still four years old, the bit that made us fumble around in bushes and school toilets, finding out what bodies were like. That's the bit of us that's brought into play when we use pornography.

MARTIN: That's the bit of you that's brought into play.

OLIVER: OK. So, I'm generalising. But isn't it true?

WILL: I think we should define what we mean by pornography, and what we mean by 'using' pornography.

OLIVER: All right. I've got us off on the wrong foot.

MARTIN: Again.

OLIVER: OK. I apologise.

BRUCE: Doesn't matter.

WILL: So. Definitions.

OLIVER: Well, I agree with the feminist argument that all pornography is based on violence against women.

WILL: Even 'Zipper'?

OLIVER: Gay porn, obviously, is different. Maybe we can discuss that separately.

MARTIN: Separatism, so soon?

OLIVER: Try and keep it serious, please, Martin.

WILL: Look, there are many different types of porn. There's straightforward Mayfair crotch shots, there's the gynaecological crotch shot. There's spanking, bondage, SM, TV, lesbianism . . .

OLIVER: For a male audience . . .

WILL: Agreed. There's straight couples, groups, animals, paedophiles. All catering to different people, to different needs. So. Do we lump them all together, and say they're all based on violence against women? Or do we try to understand if and how they differ, in content and function? And then explain if and how they may be relevant to our own lives.

Beat.

OLIVER: Are we supposed to sit here and discuss each variant in sordid bloody detail?

BRUCE: Well . . . yes . . .

WILL *gets up and takes a carrier bag from the cupboard.*

WILL: They're all in there. I bought a selection.

OLIVER: God's sake, Will . . .

WILL: Why not? If we're going to discuss it, we might as well know what we're talking about.

OLIVER: We do know . . .

WILL: And most important, if we're going to try to influence other people's rights to use porn, then we most definitely have to know. Otherwise we're just Mary Whitehouse. We must argue from experience, not prejudice.

Pause.

OLIVER: I find them offensive.

WILL: So do I. Some of them.

OLIVER: Then why do we have to look at something we know we find offensive?

WILL: Some of them, I said. (*Beat.*) I'll get the food on.

He switches off the tape and goes.

OLIVER: Do you two go along with this?

MARTIN: Why not?

BRUCE: Sure.

OLIVER: Bloody absurd. I don't need to look at these.

MARTIN: Seen it all before, eh?

OLIVER: Piss off.

MARTIN: You're embarrassed, aren't you?

OLIVER: No.

MARTIN: You can't fool me. (*He looks through the bag.*) Oh . . . My . . . God. He really went to town on this one. What d'you fancy, Ollie? 'Burning Butt' or 'Hot Ass Nurses'?

OLIVER (*more to himself*): Lose all sense of dignity. Self respect. Those things, they cheapen your soul.

MARTIN: Do wonders for your other bits, though.

OLIVER: Fuck off!

He goes out. MARTIN is a bit shaken by OLIVER's reaction.

MARTIN: He's got a stash at the flat y'know. He thinks I don't know. Keeps them at the bottom of a suitcase. (*Beat.*) How do I know? I went through his things.

BRUCE: What's he . . . into?

MARTIN: Copulating couples. (*He laughs. Pause.*) You know what I don't like about Ollie? He has 'Him' and 'Zipper' on the bookshelf, and he hides the het sex at the bottom of an old suitcase.

OLLIE *comes back in.*

OK? Not hyperventilating, or anything?

OLIVER (*mock cheerful*): No, no. Just took a deep breath and counted to ten. Works every time. Now then. (*He takes out a magazine.*) 'Lesbian Lasses.' (*He flicks through it.*) Uh huh. Women pretending to cavort together for the benefit of the male viewer. Uh huh. (*Beat. He holds it up for them to see.*) What's missing?

MARTIN: Sorry?

OLIVER: What all-important object is missing from that picture?

Beat.

MARTIN: Dunno. Toothbrush? (*He and BRUCE laugh.*)

OLIVER: No. (*Beat.*) Can't spot it? (*Beat.*) The phallus. That's what's missing. Women forced into a faked impersonation of male/female sex. Forced into behaving like men. Two women, and it's all about penetration. All it lacks is the phallus. Which is what the male reader supplies.

The door opens. ANGE, her lip now cut and swollen, comes in. OLLIE is still holding the magazine up.

Jesus . . . (*He puts it in the bag.*) I'm sorry, I wasn't . . .

ANGE: I was upstairs . . .

Beat.

OLIVER: Yeah. (*He goes to the door.*) Will? You got a minute?

They look at her. WILL appears.

WILL: Oh, Ange, hello . . . (*He sees her face.*) Bloody hell. Sit down, c'mon. (*He sits her down.*) When did you do that?

ANGE: I . . . didn't do it.

WILL: Your husband, was it? Ange? Was it your husband?

ANGE: Lenny done it.

WILL: Here? He came here?

ANGE: He came round . . . It was his dinner hour . . .

OLIVER: For Christ's sake, he comes round in his dinner hour to beat his wife up.

WILL: Yeah, OK, Ollie. Ange, is there something I can get you? That's a nasty cut.

ANGE: And he . . .

WILL: What?

ANGE: After . . .

WILL: After what?

ANGE: After he hit me . . . He . . .

WILL: What did he do after he hit you?

Beat.

BRUCE: D'you think . . . Maybe he . . . raped her . . . or something?

OLIVER: No, dear God . . .

WILL: Is that it, Ange? Did he? Did he rape you? (*She breaks down.*) Someone get a brandy, will you? (OLIVER *does.*) Here, drink some of this.

OLIVER: Should be bloody castrated.

WILL: Someone ring the centre, tell Ronee. Number's by the phone. (OLIVER *goes to the phone and dials.*)

OLIVER: We can report him, y'know. To the pigs. Get her seen by a doctor. They can put him away.

WILL (*to* ANGE): Have you been upstairs all this time? Have you? (*She nods.*) You should have come down, you daft kid.

ANGE: I's frightened.

WILL: No need to be frightened of us.

OLIVER (*into the phone*): Hello, Johnson Place? (*Beat.*) Yeah, can I speak to Ronee? (*Beat.*) Thanks. (*To* WILL:) They're getting her. (*Beat.*) Hello? Ronee? It's Oliver. From the mens' group. I'm at your house. Look, I think you'd better come home. The girl who's staying here –

WILL: Ange.

OLIVER: Yeah, Ange. Her husband's beaten her up again, and we think he might have raped her. (*Beat.*) She's in a terrible state, we don't know for sure. (*Beat.*) OK. Good. (*He puts the phone down.*) She's coming straight back.

WILL: Ronee'll be here soon, Ange. You're going to be all right. (*Beat.*) Oh fuck.

MARTIN: What's the matter?

WILL: The ribs. They'll be bloody ruined. (*He goes out.*)

OLIVER (*next to* ANGE): It's OK. You'll be OK. (*She pulls away.*) We're your friends. (*She pulls away.*) No one's going to hurt you.

ANGE: Leave me alone.

OLIVER: Hey, c'mon. We're friends of Will's.

MARTIN: Ollie . . .

OLIVER: We can help.

ANGE: Leave me alone.

OLIVER: Please.

MARTIN: Ollie.

OLIVER: What, for Christ's sake?!

BRUCE *puts his hand on* OLLIE's *shoulder.*

BRUCE: Best, maybe, leave her alone.

MARTIN: C'mon, Ollie.

OLLIE *pulls violently away from* BRUCE.

OLIVER: All right, all right.

WILL *comes back in.*

WILL: Food's fucked. Sorry.

BRUCE: 'S OK.

MARTIN: Look, why don't we go?

BRUCE: Yeah . . .

WILL: I think it's best. Sorry and all that . . .

MARTIN: Oh, come on. This is more important than our meeting. (*Pause.*) Ollie?

OLIVER: Yeah.

They get their things.

WILL: I'll call you tomorrow, work out another time.

OLIVER (*indicating the magazines*): Burn those bastard things, Will.

Beat. They go.

WILL (*to* ANGE, *who has curled up*): 'S OK, mate. Ronee won't be long. (*Beat.*) What d'you want to do? Have a sleep? (*She nods.*) I'll cover you up.

He puts his jacket over her and sits down. She closes her eyes. He goes and gets a drink and sits again.

Ange?

She seems asleep. He takes out one of the magazines and sits facing away from her. She opens her eyes and looks at him.

Fade.

Scene Four

Monday evening, 11 p.m.
WILL *is sitting in the same chair reading* Mastering the Art of French Cooking. RONEE *comes in and pours two drinks. She takes one and goes out.* WILL *carries on reading. She comes back, takes the other drink and sits down.* WILL *puts the book down and looks at her. She's very tense.*

WILL: Well?

Beat. RONEE *doesn't seem able to say what she wants to say.*

RONEE: Sod it. There are times . . . (*Beat.*) Yes. He did. And you don't have to be a doctor to see it. 'Injuries consistent with forceful sexual intercourse' is how they describe it in court. (*Beat.*) And she won't do anything about it. She won't report him.

WILL: For crying out loud . . .

RONEE: I know. But she's scared to death of him. And who wouldn't be?

Pause.

WILL: How is she now?

RONEE: She keeps waking up. That's the worst thing. It keeps coming back, apparently. (*Beat.*) It's a bloody good job Andrea's here. She knows all about it. From personal experience. (*Pause.*) She's staying tonight. (*Pause.*) You don't mind sleeping down here, do you?

WILL: No. (*Meaning yes.*)

Pause.

RONEE (*after a nervous laugh*): I just don't know if Ange could handle it. If she woke up. And saw a man . . .

WILL: It's OK. It really is.

Pause.

RONEE: All in all, this has been a bastard day. Two kids had a fight at the Centre. Girls. Using those Afro combs, y'know. (*Beat.*) I tell you, I despair sometimes.

WILL: Don't.

RONEE: I'm tired. That's all.

WILL: You sure?

RONEE: What d'you mean?

Beat.

WILL: Are you *just* tired?

RONEE: I don't understand.

WILL: Neither do I. (*Beat.*) Sorry. I didn't mean to lay that on you.

RONEE: Forget it. (*Pause.*) I know I've been a bit . . . distant lately. I can't help it. Work and everything . . .

WILL: And Andrea . . .

RONEE: Yes. And Andrea. (*Pause.*) Don't forget you encouraged me. It was actually your idea.

WILL: It wasn't my idea that you'd have a completely independent affair.

RONEE: No, what you wanted was a happy little set-up where you got your kicks whenever you felt like it, without any involvement. And I can't do that. I have to invest a piece of *me* in people I sleep with. I can't just do it and – I dunno – tape record it and play it back. I'm not that detached.

WILL: I wanted to try something a bit radical. I'm sorry you couldn't handle it.

RONEE: There's nothing radical about a harem.

WILL: Bullshit, Ronee. That's not what I wanted. I wanted to try other ways of keeping a relationship alive.

RONEE: Our relationship wasn't dead.

WILL: And it is now?

RONEE: I don't know. (*Beat.*) You're forever meddling with people. You're never content just to be, and let other people be. You have to keep fiddling about, trying new things. And it doesn't work.

Pause.

WILL: And your little lesbian affair isn't 'fiddling about'? That works, does it?

RONEE: Don't say 'little lesbian affair' like that. You were happy enough when we let you in. And yes, it does work. Now that you're not involved, it works. Like a dream.

Pause.

WILL: This is political lesbianism we're talking about, isn't it? It's nothing to do with sex. You'd prefer to keep sex right out of it. Because sex can be dangerous. You can't always control it. Sometimes it turns wild on you. And you don't go too near things you don't understand, do you? 'O Lord, spare us the unpredictable.' That's your prayer.

RONEE: Unpredictable? You? You inflict a few dippy ideas on me and Andrea, a few dusty clichés you've got hanging around from the sixties and that's supposed to indicate a wild, dangerous nature, is it? You: a progressive free spirit? (*Beat.*) Well, the reason we exclude you is that it had become a cliché. There's nothing wild or dangerous about a live sex show, although you might disagree. And that's all we were. You put your penny in the slot, and we'd perform. For you. For your entertainment. We got absolutely nothing from it, except the growing realisation that if you weren't there, then there was maybe something we could find together. For ourselves. Just ourselves. (*Beat.*) You're right. It was unpredictable. It was dangerous. For you. (*Pause.*) You wanted cheap thrills, and you got 'em. But you paid. (*A door slams.*) I'm very tired, Will. I'm sorry.

MARK *puts his head round the door.*

MARK: Yo. All right if I come in?

WILL: Yeah, I want to have a word.

MARK (*coming in*): Christ, have I had a day. I finally collared this fella, this singer, and I said, 'Given that you've denied in print that you're a screaming woofter, how d'you account for the little Filipino back-door boy you've had in your trendy mews flat all night?' And he says 'Are you pulling my plonker! I don't know what you're on about.' At which point, said Filipino bum-bandit tries to make it away out the back. Well, immortalised forever by the process of photographic impression, isn't he? So, man with the golden tonsils cracks up, rings his manager and agrees to exclusive interview in which he admits that he may just have indulged in some male willy-stretching in the dim and murky past, but that's all behind him, 'scuse the pun. And anyway he's thinking of becoming a Christian. (*Beat.*) Mission accomplished. Am I a reptile, or what?

RONEE: You're disgusting.

MARK (*smiling*): Mmm. (*Pause. To* WILL:) Hey, ask me how many feminists it takes to screw in a lightbulb. Go on. Ask me.

WILL: Get lost, Mark.

MARK: Come on. How many feminists does it take? Ask me.

Beat.

WILL (*reluctantly*): How many feminists does it take to screw in a . . .

MARK (*mock strident, pointing his finger*): That's not funny! (*He laughs.*) Heard that one today.

WILL *stands.*

WILL (*to* RONEE): I'm going for a walk. Get some chips. You can tell him . . .

RONEE: Yeah.

WILL *goes.*

MARK: Just you and me, eh? Cosy.

RONEE: Shut your sexist trap for two seconds, will you?

MARK: I love it when you talk dirty.

RONEE: Like banging your head against a brick wall . . .

MARK: I'm not fussy. Brick wall, chandelier, wardrobe, you name it, I'll bang against it.

RONEE: Stop! While I talk to you, I'll be brief. I won't overtax your powers of concentration, I promise. I just want your undivided attention for two seconds, OK?

MARK: What are you doing for the rest of your life?

RONEE: OK?

MARK: Fixed up for breakfast, are you? (*Pause.*) All right.

Beat.

RONEE: Did you meet Ange? She stayed last night.

MARK: Told you, has she?

RONEE: Told me what?

MARK: That she finds me irresistible.

RONEE: You've met her, then?

MARK: I should cocoa. Blood pressure's been up all day. Amongst other things.

RONEE: Sometime today her husband came round and . . .

MARK: Yeah, I met him.

WILL: When?

MARK: Lunchtime. I came back for my address book. Seemed a nice enough fella.

RONEE: What was he doing?

MARK: Er . . . having a cup of tea.

Beat.

RONEE: Well, I presume after you'd gone, your nice enough fella beat up and raped his wife.

MARK: Get away.

Beat.

RONEE: Bloody hell, you're sympathetic . . . Anyway, the thing is, she's in a dreadful state, so: one, be as quiet as you can, and two, don't give her any of your hilarious scatalogical badinage. Cut the sexist crap, all right?

Beat.

MARK: Never entered your head, has it, that all this linguistic and ideological purity – don't forget I've got a degree too – is just a little bit arrogant?

RONEE: If you weren't so crass I wouldn't have to keep telling you.

MARK: And if you didn't keep telling me, then maybe I wouldn't be so crass. (*Beat.*) Think about it.

Beat.

RONEE: I've got someone else staying the night, too. A friend of mine. Pinch her bum and she's likely to cut your throat. You think about that.

MARK: I don't pinch bums. I admire them.

RONEE: Whatever.

Pause. She gets blankets and a pillow from the cupboard and spreads them on the sofa.

MARK: Well, really, I'm not that kind of boy. (*No response.*) You wind yourself up any tighter, you're going to snap. (*Beat.*)

G'night. And don't forget to leave that window open . . .

He laughs and goes. She takes a deep breath and finishes making up the bed. Then switches out the main light. As she's about to go, the doorbell rings.

RONEE: Why didn't you take your keys . . . ?

She goes. We hear talking and suddenly LENNY *appears with* RONEE *following. He's totally legless.*

LENNY: Where you got her? Eh?

RONEE: I said out! Now!

LENNY: Upstairs, is she? With that bloke? That cunt?

She shuts the door.

RONEE: If you go out of this room, it's to go out the front door, OK?

LENNY: Listen, you fucking cow, I wanna see Ange.

RONEE: You can't. She's not here.

LENNY: Fuck off.

RONEE: She's where you put her. In the hospital.

LENNY: What you talking about? Get fucked. I wanna see my wife. (*Pause. He sees the drinks and takes a bottle of gin and swigs from it.*)

RONEE: You've had enough to drink.

LENNY: I've only had eleven fucking pints. (*He takes a huge swig. As he drinks, we see him quickly become less and less capable.*)

RONEE: If you don't go, I'm calling the police.

LENNY: Fucking try it.

RONEE: I'm warning you.

LENNY: Shove it up your middle class fucking arsehole, fucking bitch. (*He takes a huge swig, then takes a bottle of scotch and drinks from that. He takes his poem out of his pocket.*) Hey, listen. This is what I wrote. Didn't think I could fucking write, did you? Well I can. Listen. 'When I look up at the sky/And the clouds are floating by/I think about you/And the things you do. When the sun comes out/ It makes me want to shout/Your name out loud/To the passing crowd. When it starts to rain/I can feel the pain/That's going to come/Now that you're gone.' Yeah. I fucking wrote that.

RONEE: Yeah. Very nice . . .

LENNY: But I've written another one. 'Cause I reckon that one's fucking stupid. This one's better. (*He reads:*) 'When I get my hands on you/I'm gonna put my fingers round your throat/And squeeze till you go blue. I'm gonna write on your face/With a razor blade/I'm Lenny and I love you. I'm gonna slice your tits/And slash your fanny/And cut your tongue out too. I'm gonna drop you in the river/With your head cut off/And a note saying I love you.'

He takes a swig and stands staring at the floor, completely preoccupied. RONEE goes to the phone and picks it up. He moves towards her, and, as she puts the phone down, raises his arm to give her a backhander. As his arm comes down, she blocks it karate style and hits him hard in the stomach. He drops, retching, throws up and passes out. Door slams. WILL enters, puts the light on, and sees them. He's eating a bag of chips.

Will, Lenny. Lenny, Will.

Beat.

WILL: Hello, Lenny.

Beat.

RONEE: Passed out.

WILL: Mmm. (*Beat.*) Fancy a chip?

Blackout.

ACT TWO

Scene One

Monday morning, 10 a.m.
   A week later. ANGE *is lying on the sofa.* MARK *is at the table reading the paper, eating toast and drinking coffee. They're ignoring each other.* RONEE *enters.*

RONEE: What bright spark left the hot tap running in the bathroom?

MARK *looks at her then at* ANGE.

Ange . . .

ANGE: What?

RONEE: Love, try to get it together, will you? Please?

ANGE: I never left it on.

RONEE: Taps don't turn themselves on.

ANGE: I never.

RONEE: OK . . .

MARK *stands with his cup.*

MARK: Round the bloody twist.

He goes.

RONEE: You going to make it to the Centre today?

ANGE: Dunno.

RONEE: I wish you'd try. (*Pause.*) I'll wait if you want to come now. (ANGE *shakes her head.*) Look, we'll have a talk. You can't go on like this.

ANGE: I have talked.

RONEE: I know.

ANGE: Fed up with talking.

RONEE: It's for your own good. (*Beat.*) You've got to get back into it. You can't stay here indefinitely.

ANGE: Why not?

Beat.

RONEE: Look, Will and I are having some problems. We need to sort ourselves out. And it's not very easy . . . Y'know.

ANGE: 'Cause of me.

RONEE: No, not because of you.

ANGE: What about Andrea?

RONEE: What do you mean?

MARK *enters with a cup of coffee.*

We'll talk about it later. See you.

She goes.

MARK: Give me half an hour, I could sort all your problems out. (*Pause.*) Milking it a bit, don't you think? (*Pause.*) You like it here. I can tell. I wonder why? (*He goes over to her.*) What are you after?

ANGE: Nothing.

MARK: Think I'm stupid, do you?

ANGE: Yeah.

MARK: Be making a silly mistake, you go around thinking that. (*Pause.*) Why don't you come out for a drink with me. (*Beat.*) Take you somewhere a bit classy. Wine bar. Cocktail bar. You'd like that. (*Pause.*) No? (*Pause.*) You've got a fantastic body. (*Beat.*) Look at me. (*She does.*) I mean . . . You could do worse.

ANGE: You reckon?

MARK: Much worse. See I'm not the sort of fella who fiddles about with little girls' minds.

ANGE: No, I know what you fiddle about with.

MARK: I'm good at it, too.

ANGE: I'll bet.

Pause.

MARK: So. Try it?

ANGE: Up yours.

MARK: You should be so lucky. (*Pause. He gets up and goes back to the table.*) I might start exercising my tenants' rights, y'know. You're not exactly my idea of a positive addition to the household, if you know what I mean. I might have to complain.

ANGE: All the bloody same, ain't you?

MARK: Yeah. Deep down. I suppose we are.

WILL *enters in his dressing-gown.*

WILL: Morning.

MARK: Morning.

ANGE: Hello, Will.

WILL: Ange.

Beat.

MARK: Here, media joke. You'll like this one, it's about your lot. How many feminists does it take . . .

WILL: You've told me.

MARK: It's a new one. How many feminists does it take to screw in a lightbulb?

WILL: I don't know.

MARK: Thirty-six. One to screw in the lightbulb and thirty-five to make a documentary of it for Channel Four.

WILL: That's not funny.

MARK: Loosen up, pal.

ANGE *gets up.*

ANGE: D'you want some tea, Will?

WILL: Thanks.

MARK: Do us some coffee.

ANGE: You know where the kitchen is.

She goes.

MARK: Obviously, I don't have your charisma.

WILL: Obviously.

Pause.

MARK: Being a bit naughty, aren't we?

WILL: Who is?

Beat.

MARK: You given her one yet?

WILL: What are you talking about?

MARK: Simple question.

WILL: From a simple mind. You've got to reduce everything, haven't you? Drag it all down to the gutter. Well, for your information, Ange has been through a pretty rotten experience, and what she needs is support. That's the only thing I've given her. Support. Human warmth. A couple of things you know nothing about.

MARK: I know about quite a few things. You'd be surprised.

WILL: Such as?

Pause

MARK: She's using you as much as you're using her.

Beat.

WILL: You're a walking insult, you know that? It's not just progressive ideas you can't cope with, it's basic human relationships as well. Just because you think with your prick, you imagine we all do. (*Beat.*) It must be a pretty weird experience, seeing, feeling everything from only that high above the ground. (*He gestures at groin level.*) I'll tell you what, you should trade in that nice company Volvo you drive. You'd be happier swinging through the trees.

MARK: Nice one.

WILL: Well, wouldn't you?

MARK: Bollocks. You know your trouble? You can't change your socks without pretending you're changing the world.

WILL: You just don't understand, do you?

MARK: Don't be so piss-arrogant.

WILL: Don't be so thick.

ANGE *comes in with a cup of tea and gives it to* WILL.

ANGE: Here y'are.

WILL: Thanks.

MARK *gets his jacket and case.*

MARK: You'll be late for work.

WILL: Got the morning off.

MARK: Yeah. Figures.

He laughs and goes.

WILL: Has he been giving you a hard time?

ANGE: Not really.

WILL: Tell me if he does.

ANGE: Yeah. (*Beat.*) He said I had a fantastic body.

WILL: I'm sorry. Look, if he does it again . . .

ANGE: 'S OK. I don't mind.

WILL: You should do. Fantastic body. Christ, that's all he can see, isn't it?

ANGE: Don't worry about it.

WILL: I can't help it. I just do. (*Pause.*) It just seems to me sometimes, that all that's required is the tiniest amount of thought. If we all, suddenly, one day said, 'Yeah, OK, I'll try it.' All at once. Then . . . And

it could happen. It would happen. (*Pause.*) Not like me to be optimistic first thing in the morning. I'd better see a doctor. (*She smiles.*) That's better.

ANGE: You're funny.

WILL: I'm not quite sure how to take that.

ANGE: You think about everything all the time. I never know what you're gonna say next.

WILL: Me neither.

ANGE: That's not true. You got an answer for everything.

WILL: If only. (*Pause.*) Ange. D'you think of me as old?

ANGE: You what?

WILL: Do I seem . . . a lot older, to you?

ANGE: Never thought about it.

Pause.

WILL: I was in grammar school, fourteen, studying for O-levels the day you were born. All acne and pubertal angst.

ANGE: Sounds filthy.

WILL: It probably was.

Pause.

ANGE: You're only as young as you feel. That's what they say, isn't it?

WILL: Is it?

ANGE: Yeah.

WILL: Well, then . . .

ANGE: How old do you feel? (*Beat.*)

WILL: Eighteen . . . Eighty . . . It varies.

ANGE: Stick with eighteen if I was you.

WILL: What, never grow up?

ANGE: No, never.

WILL: I'll think about it.

ANGE: No, don't think about it. Just do it.

Pause.

WILL: You didn't answer my question

ANGE: Which one?

WILL: D'you think I'm old?

ANGE: I don't think about it.

WILL: Very diplomatic.

ANGE: I don't.

Beat.

WILL: 'Course, the main danger in feeling old, is that you start getting boring about it. Let me know if I'm boring you.

ANGE: You're not.

WILL: And you don't have to be polite.

ANGE: Wouldn't know how.

WILL: You're not daft.

ANGE: Ain't got no O-levels.

WILL: Some of the daftest people I know are graduates. Including me.

ANGE: Well *you* ain't daft.

WILL: No?

ANGE: 'Course not.

WILL: Shows how little you know me. (*The doorbell rings.*) Who the bloody hell's that?

He goes to the door. We hear muffled voices. OLIVER comes in followed by WILL.

OLIVER: I rang your office. They said you wouldn't be in today. Hope you don't mind.

WILL: No.

OLIVER: Hi, Ange.

ANGE: Wotcher.

WILL: You look bloody terrible, mate.

OLIVER: I've been up all night.

WILL: Problems?

OLIVER: Since when did I have anything else?

WILL: Martin?

OLIVER: Oh, yes. Very much. Martin.

ANGE: Shall I do some tea?

WILL: Great idea. Ta.

OLIVER: Coffee for me.

She goes.

I'm sorry, Will. I just don't know who to turn to.

WILL: Come on, it's OK. (*Beat.*) So what's happening?

OLIVER: Jesus, where do I start. (*Beat.*)

Basically, I haven't seen him for two days. See, I gave him a sort of ultimatum. Yeah. I know. Pretty naff, right? Standing there in my curlers, with the rolling pin. Not exactly progressive, I know. But. Like. I had to do something. I mean, we're falling apart. Our so-called relationship is just about ready for the knacker's yard.

WILL: It happens.

OLIVER: Sure, it happens. Happens all the time. All over the world. (*Pause.*) Will, *why?*

Long pause.

WILL: Lots of reasons, Ollie. Depends on the people.

Pause.

OLIVER: When my ex-wife left me, I said, right, that's it. I am never again going to get myself stung like that. Never. I don't care what it takes. I'll never again put myself in a position where one person can single-handedly dismantle my life. Y'know? (*Beat.*) You build it up, slowly . . . (*Beat.*) Like the business . . . I mean, I've put everything into that stall. Even started thinking about getting premises. A shop. Yeah. A shop. Hip capitalism. Well, I haven't made or sold a thing all week. I can't. It's just collapsing. I'm paralysed. (*Pause.*) Martin. I thought, it'll never turn out like it did with Marie, my ex-wife. I won't let it. This is different. Martin's a guy, for chrissakes. He won't do that to me. (*Pause.*) Will. We don't have sex. I know we pretend . . . I mean, it's not that we don't want to, it's just . . . It's another complication. And Martin knew that. The ad I put in Time Out, it said, 'Guy wants guy for friendship.' That's all. All. Christ, isn't it enough? Doesn't anybody want to be friends in this world any more?

Pause.

WILL: Ollie . . . Maybe Martin didn't like the pretence.

OLIVER: Maybe Martin just wanted to get his rotten little end away. Maybe Martin doesn't give a damn if he fucks our relationship up. (*Pause.*) And maybe Martin didn't like the pretence. Shit. Pretence? Let's not kid ourselves. Lies, Will. What it boils down to. Lies.

ANGE *comes in with tea and coffee on a tray and puts it down.*

ANGE: I'll . . .

WILL: Yeah.

OLIVER: Thanks. For the coffee.

ANGE: 'S OK.

She goes.

OLIVER: I've realised it too late, haven't I?

WILL: Maybe.

OLIVER: Why do I find it so hard to admit the truth? Marie once said to me that, when I died, I'd refuse to lie down and admit it. Why do I find it so hard?

WILL: We all do, don't we?

OLIVER: Do you? Even you?

Pause.

WILL: Yes. (*Pause.*) Look . . . Don't despair. (*Pause.*) Sorry. That's all I can say. If Martin's gone for good, then you'll have to adjust.

OLIVER: Have you ever been lonely, Will?

WILL: Yeah . . .

OLIVER: I mean . . . *Lonely. Alone.* (*Beat.*) I've gone days without talking to another person. Whole days of drinking coffee, pretending to work, drinking a bottle of scotch. All in total silence. God, I hate silence. (*Beat.*) One of the things . . . About Martin: he talks a lot. I like that. I always dry his hair for him when he's had a shower. And we babble. Nothing in particular, y'know. Chat about the weather. You've got split ends, that's a nice shirt . . . (*Pause.*) Sorry. (*Pause.*) It's why I hate the country. The silence. It frightens me. (*Beat.*) Have you ever tried listening to the radio? When you're alone?

WILL: Sure.

OLIVER: I don't really mean *when* you're alone, I mean *because* you're alone. Anything to fill the gap. I always do it. And it makes it worse. Well-bred voice, sort of hanging in the middle of the room. I look at the radio, and I think, there's nobody fucking there. (*Pause.*) I remember a rainy afternoon. My mother doing the ironing. The smell of clean shirts. And the radio on.

Pause.

WILL: He might come back.

OLIVER: Don't know if I want him back. (*Beat.*) Of course I bloody want him back. He's all I've got.

WILL: Have you tried to find him?

OLIVER: Where? I don't know any of his friends. I wouldn't know where to start. I just have to sit and wait.

WILL: I'd offer to let you stay here, but . . .

OLIVER: No, no. I want to be there if he comes back.

WILL: And if he doesn't?

OLIVER: I suppose I'll just . . . be there.

Pause.

WILL: You're still coming round tonight, aren't you?

OLIVER: Yeah. He might turn up.

WILL: That's what I was thinking. Look on the bright side.

OLIVER: Yeah. (*Beat.*) Will. You're a good man. Thanks

WILL: Any time.

OLIVER: Say goodbye to Ange for me.

WILL: Will do.

OLIVER: See myself out.

He goes. ANGE *comes in.*

ANGE: Funny little bloke, inne?

Beat.

WILL: Yeah. Funny little bloke. (*Beat.*) I don't know what it is, but something about him . . . makes me very angry.

ANGE: Why?

WILL: I wish I knew.

Pause.

ANGE: Have you had some breakfast?

WILL: Angela. Stop doing things for me.

ANGE: Have you?

WILL: Had some muesli when I got up.

ANGE: Rabbit food. You'll turn into a rabbit. He's like a rabbit. Or a mouse. (*Pause.*) Lenny always has a cooked breakfast. Bacon, sausage, fried slice. And he covers it in HP sauce. Then he goes out. And all day there's this smell . . . Grease . . . all round the flat. I open the windows, keep washing my face, but it just stays there. All day. (*Pause.*) Why ain't you at work then?

WILL: Basically, I'm skiving.

ANGE: You'll get the sack.

WILL: But I'm pretending I'm working. Nobody knows.

Pause.

ANGE: What you gonna do all day then?

WILL: Lounge around. Read a book. I dunno. Have a think.

Beat.

ANGE: You and Ronee . . .

WILL: What?

Beat.

ANGE: You having a barney?

WILL: We don't have barneys. We have orgies of socio-political truth-telling.

ANGE: Maybe you should have a barney.

WILL: Maybe you're right

Pause.

ANGE: She must be mad . . .

WILL: Why?

ANGE: Bloke like you. One in a million. (WILL *laughs.*) What's funny?

WILL: I'm not very different.

ANGE: I think you are.

WILL: Well, thank you very much.

ANGE: Don't muck about. I do.

Beat.

WILL: If only you knew.

ANGE: What?

WILL: What a . . . mucky sort of person I am. You'd find I'm the same as anyone else. Worse.

ANGE: No.

WILL *sits and plays with the backgammon set open on the table.*

D'you want a game?

WILL: Didn't know you played.

ANGE: Ronee showed me. Not very good though.

WILL: OK. I'll give you a thrashing.

ANGE: You good at this, are you?

WILL: Pretty good. Used to be the strip backgammon king of Sussex University. That's the smutty version. If one of your counters gets taken off, you take off an article of clothing.

ANGE: Like strip poker.

WILL: Yeah. Anyway throw for start. (*They throw.*) You go first. (*She throws and moves. He throws and moves. She throws again.*) Oh dear.

She moves two counters, both uncovered. He throws and smiles.

Sorry about that.

He takes one of her counters off. Pause.

ANGE: We playing the smutty version?

WILL: If you like.

Blackout.

Scene Two

Monday evening, 6.30 p.m.
   ANGE *is polishing the table, singing to herself.* RONEE *enters, sees her and smiles.*

RONEE: Well.

ANGE (*very cheery*): Hi.

RONEE: What are *you* on?

ANGE: Come again?

RONEE: You been at the gin?

ANGE: Don't drink. You know that.

RONEE: First time I've seen you smile in days.

ANGE: Not against the law, is it?

RONEE: No. Definitely not.

Pause.

ANGE: I've cleaned upstairs and the kitchen.

RONEE: Thanks. You don't have to, y'know.

ANGE: I wanted to.

RONEE: Fine by me. (*Beat.*) God, I think I'll have a drink. (*She pours a sherry.*) Had a finance committee meeting this afternoon. Council want to cut our grant.

Not a lot. Just enough. Enough to make running the place an even bigger headache. I've got to try and decide which is more important: amplifier for the music workshop, or a new ping pong table. And they call this creative administration. Pretty soon, y'know, the only activities we'll be putting on will be benefits. Save the Centre. Rock for a new ping pong table. That kind of thing.

ANGE: Councils are stupid. Trouble we had getting our flat. Like the football league, Lenny said. We never had enough points. When the bloke came round, Lenny asked him if we was gonna get relegated to the second division. The bloke laughed and said, far as the council's concerned, we're division four. Yeah. What a pig.

RONEE: It's not their fault. Well, not all of them. The orders came from on high. I vos only oabyink orders, jawohl. (ANGE *laughs*.) Shall we have that talk now?

Pause.

ANGE: If you like.

RONEE: Come and sit down. (ANGE *sits next to her on the sofa*.) Right.

ANGE: 'S like being back at school.

RONEE: Hey, do me a favour.

ANGE: Sorry.

Beat.

RONEE: First, what are you going to do about Lenny?

ANGE: Dunno. Shoot him?

RONEE: An attractive, if impractical, suggestion. No. Are you intending to go back to him?

ANGE: You gotta be joking.

RONEE: OK. So that's out. It's separation, then. Where are you going to live? (*Pause*.) Ange?

ANGE: What?

RONEE: Where are you going to live?

ANGE: Dunno.

RONEE: Your mum's?

ANGE: Could do.

RONEE: You've got to think about it.

ANGE: Well, I thought that . . .

The phone rings.

RONEE: Shit. Hang on a minute. (*She picks up the phone*.) Hello? (*Beat*.) Oh, hi. (*Pause*.) Ja. Nach zwei Stunde. (*Beat*.) Oh. (*She laughs*.) But my pronunciation's improving. (*Beat. She laughs again*.) Rat. Schwein. (*Beat*.) Ja. Ich werde dich dahin gesehen. (*Beat*.) What? (*Beat*.) I'm trying to say I'll see you there in a couple of hours. (*Beat*.) Well I think it'd be easier if you learned English, so there. (*Beat*.) Ja. OK. Ich liebe dich. Wiedersehen. (*She puts down the phone*.) That woman is totally crazy.

ANGE: Andrea?

RONEE: Well, I don't talk to my mother in German, do I? (ANGE *shrugs*.) Right, where were we?

ANGE: Ronee? Can I ask you something?

RONEE: Trying to get off the subject?

ANGE: I want to ask you something.

RONEE: Go on then.

Beat.

ANGE: You and Andrea . . . When you . . .

RONEE: And stop it right there. If you were going to ask what I think you were going to ask, the answer is: none of your bloody business.

ANGE: I was just . . .

RONEE: Curious. Well, use your imagination.

ANGE: I mean, I can't imagine . . .

RONEE: So don't. (*Pause*.) Sorry, love. It's just that my relationship with Andrea is private and personal, y'know? I don't like it being . . . spied on.

ANGE: I wasn't spying . . .

RONEE: I know. Just curious. (*Pause*.) I don't think I could describe it, anyway.

ANGE: But . . . It's different, innit?

RONEE: Yes. It's very different.

ANGE: Better?

RONEE: For me, yeah.

Beat.

ANGE: What about Will? (*Beat*.) Don't you like him?

RONEE: We're married.

ANGE: So am I, and I don't like Lenny.

RONEE: They're very similar, Will and Lenny.

ANGE: Get off.

RONEE: Oh, I know, one's a TV researcher, the other's a mechanic; one went to University, the other left school at sixteen. But they're both men. And very similar ones at that.

ANGE: I think that's horrible. Will's nice.

Pause.

RONEE: Will is evil. (*Beat.*) And that's it. No more. There's nothing he'd like more than to think that we were sitting here talking about him. Bit of an egomaniac, is our Will.

WILL *enters with* BRUCE. *They've been mending the car and are both covered in oil. They each have a can of beer and two more unopened.*

WILL: You called?

RONEE: Done it?

WILL: Not quite. Got to bleed the brakes. Thought we'd have a quick beer. So. Talking about me?

RONEE: Pick it up on your radar, did you? Someone, somewhere, says 'Will' and a little bleep appears on the screen?

WILL: Something like that.

RONEE: I was just disabusing Ange of a rather peculiar notion she had. She seems to have been labouring under the misapprehension that you are nice.

WILL: But you put her straight.

RONEE: Of course, dear heart.

WILL: You're a treasure.

WILL *crushes his empty can.*

RONEE: I know. (*Beat.*) God, this is all too macho for me. I've got to get changed, anyway. Come on, Ange, we can carry on talking. I intend to get you sorted out. (*She stands.*)

WILL: Come along, Angela. Walkies.

RONEE: Let's leave the boys to their beer and motor cars.

She and ANGE *go.*

WILL: Ain't she sweet? (*Beat.*) Never get married, Bruce.

BRUCE: I . . . won't.

Pause.

WILL: Hey, listen, mate, thanks for your help. That car's been a pain in the arse since I bought it. I'd never have got it straight if you hadn't come over.

BRUCE: No problem. I . . . enjoy it.

Beat. WILL *as always, is uncomfortable with* BRUCE.

WILL: You can take a shower later, if you want.

BRUCE: 'S OK. You've got some . . . uh . . . Swarfega . . .

WILL: Yeah. I'll get it . . .

BRUCE: No, I'll . . . finish this . . . (*He holds up his beer.*)

WILL: Sure. (*Pause.*) So.

Beat.

BRUCE: You don't have to . . . talk. If you don't want to.

WILL: Bit pre-occupied, that's all.

BRUCE: Ah.

WILL: Ronee and me. Well, you can probably see . . . We're not . . . I dunno . . .

BRUCE: Maybe you should split.

Beat.

WILL: Does it look that bad?

BRUCE: Doesn't . . . look good.

WILL: No. (*Pause.*) Rationally . . . you're probably right. But who thinks rationally at times like this? (*Pause.*) Ten years we've been together. Married for six. Very unfashionable, marriage, when we did it. Which is probably why we did it. (*Beat.*) Ten years. (*Beat.*) That . . . is a bloody long time.

Pause.

BRUCE: I've got a flat.

WILL: Good news. Where?

BRUCE: Earl's Court. Sharing.

WILL: Who with?

BRUCE: Couple of . . . blokes I know . . .

WILL: That's you sorted out, then.

BRUCE: Yeah.

The doorbell rings.

WILL: I'll get it.

He goes to the door. There are muffled voices. MARTIN *comes in, followed by* WILL.

Drink?

MARTIN: Yeah. Gin. On its own. (*He glowers at* BRUCE. BRUCE *ignores him and sips his beer.*)

WILL: There you go. (*He hands him his drink.*) Cheers. (MARTIN *drinks most of it down in one go.*) So. You're early.

Beat.

MARTIN: Yeah.

Beat.

WILL: To what do we owe the pleasure? (*Pause.*) Well, it's OK. Since you're here. Know anything about cars?

MARTIN: No.

WILL: Oh, well. (*Pause.*) Ollie was round this morning.

MARTIN: Oh, Christ . . .

WILL: He was . . . in a bit of a bad way.

MARTIN: What else is fucking new?

WILL: He was worried about you. (*Pause.*) Have you seen him?

MARTIN: No.

WILL: Not to worry. He'll be here soon. He's usually early. (*Pause.*) Look, Martin . . .

MARTIN (*to* BRUCE): What the fuck are you playing at? (*Pause.* WILL *is baffled.*) Come on. It's only a speech defect. You're not dumb.

BRUCE, *very calmly, goes over to* MARTIN *and suddenly grabs the hair on the back of his neck. It is very painful.*

BRUCE (*speaking carefully so as not to stammer*): Don't ever speak to me like that. OK? (*He lets go.*)

WILL: Er . . . I get the feeling there's something I'm missing here. (*Pause.*) But . . . Maybe the penny's dropping.

Pause.

BRUCE: Can I have another . . . beer?

WILL: Oh, help yourself.

BRUCE *does as* MARTIN *takes a piece of paper out of his pocket.*

MARTIN: I mean, what is this?

Beat.

WILL: Looks like a piece of paper to me . . .

MARTIN (*reading*): 'Dear Martin, I've moved. Don't try to find me. Don't come round. Goodbye. Thanks. Bruce.' (*Pause.*) I mean, y'know . . .

WILL: Sounds like the brush-off to me.

Pause.

MARTIN: Bruce?

Beat.

BRUCE: Sounds like . . . the brush-off to me, too.

MARTIN: But why?

BRUCE: I got bored.

MARTIN: You what?!

WILL: He got bored.

Pause.

MARTIN: Jesus Christ, what have I done?

WILL: Tell you one thing: you've made a little man very unhappy, for a start.

MARTIN: Please, Will, I think this is between me and Bruce.

WILL: So go to your place to discuss it. (*Beat.*) Look, Ollie was here in what I can only describe as a mess, this morning. A mess on your account. You appear to be in a mess on Bruce's account. Why don't you and Ollie get your respective messes together and live happily ever after?

MARTIN: Don't patronise me, you sod.

WILL: I wish there was a way not to. I wish it wasn't inevitable. (*Beat.*) You, and Ollie, what is it you're always on the verge of? Huh? You're always teetering on the brink. The brink of what?

Beat.

MARTIN: The same as you.

WILL: Cryptic.

MARTIN: You know what I mean.

WILL: Enlighten me.

MARTIN: What are you going to do when Ronee leaves you?

Beat.

WILL: Oh, oh, oh, I see what you're driving at.

MARTIN: Not going to teeter on the brink? Huh?

WILL (*arch*): I'll burn that bridge when I come to it. Until then, let's remember that it's my private affair.

MARTIN: Oh, so cool.

WILL: If by that you mean that I don't wank my private life all over other people's boots, then you're dead right. (*Pause.*) It's just occurred to me. We shouldn't be having this discussion. We're not quorate and we haven't got a chairperson.

BRUCE *laughs.*

MARTIN: Bruce?

BRUCE: It was fun. That's . . . all.

Beat.

MARTIN: OK. (*He gets up and starts to pour a drink.*)

WILL: I'm really going to have to think about setting up a drinks kitty. (MARTIN *pulls a pound note out of his pocket and throws it in* WILL'*s direction.*) All I meant was – ask.

MARTIN (*having poured*): May I?

WILL: Be my guest.

MARTIN *goes to* BRUCE *and theatrically throws the drink in his face. Beat.* BRUCE *starts to laugh, as does* WILL. *As they laugh* BRUCE *indicates that he's going to the bathroom. He goes, still laughing.*

You definitely get tonight's Joan Crawford award.

MARTIN *is nearly in tears.*

Think about it. He's only doing what you did to Ollie.

MARTIN: I know. (*Pause.*) Except, Bruce and me . . .

WILL: Yeah. (*Beat. He goes to the window.*) Beautiful day. (*Beat.*) I've got an idea. Let's have a barbeque.

MARTIN: What, now?

WILL: I'll have to go and get some mince . . . (*He goes to the door.*) Ronee?

RONEE (*off*): Yeah?

WILL: What time are you back tonight?

RONEE (*off*): Not late.

WILL: I've got an idea.

RONEE (*off*): Golly.

WILL: What about a barbeque in the garden? (*Beat.*) Eh?

RONEE (*off*): Yeah. Great.

WILL: You back by half nine?

Beat.

RONEE (*off*): I suppose so.

WILL: OK. Bring Andrea, if you like. (*Beat. He comes back into the room.*) It'll be beautiful out there tonight. Just right.

ANGE *appears.*

ANGE: Need any help?

WILL: Uh . . . Not really. I've got to get to the shop . . .

ANGE: I'll go.

WILL: 'S OK. I want to get out. (*Beat.*) Come with me, if you like.

ANGE: Yeah.

WILL: Know anything about barbeques?

ANGE: What, hot dogs and stuff?

WILL: I was thinking more in terms of burgers and kebabs.

ANGE: You can show me.

WILL: OK. (*Beat.*) See you later.

MARTIN: Yeah.

They start to go as BRUCE *comes in.*

WILL: Just going to the shop, Bruce.

BRUCE: I'll finish the car.

MARTIN: Bruce.

WILL *and* ANGE *go.*

Sorry. I made a fool of myself.(*Beat.*) I'm apologising. Say something.

BRUCE: What?

MARTIN: I don't know.

Pause.

BRUCE: The only . . . creatures on this earth worth pitying . . . are animals. Cause, like . . . people . . . y'know? People are so stupid. They're . . . happy with all their crap . . . Like . . . They don't want to get any better. (*Beat.*) Politics is a joke. People don't want to be . . . liberated. I think people . . . like being chained up. Not real chains . . . Y'know. Keep those for the animals.

Pause.

MARTIN (*sings gently*): Chains, my baby's got me locked up in chains. And they ain't the kind . . . that you can see . . .

Pause. The doorbell rings. BRUCE goes. OLIVER enters. MARTIN sees him and carries on singing:

Whoah-oh these chains of love, gotta hold on me.

Beat.

OLIVER: Are you pissed? (*MARTIN shakes his head.*) What's Bruce doing?

MARTIN: Mending Will's car.

Pause.

OLIVER (*sitting*): Martin . . . (*Beat.*) Where have you been?

RONEE *comes in.*

RONEE: Boy scout night again already?

OLIVER: Hi, Ronee.

RONEE: Hi. Look, if you bump into my husband, tell him I'll do my best to be back in time, will you?

OLIVER: Sure.

RONEE: But, I can't promise.

OLIVER: OK.

She goes.

In time for what?

MARTIN: It'll be beautiful out there tonight.

OLIVER: Eh?

MARTIN: We're having a barbeque in the garden. Songs round the old campfire.

OLIVER: What for?

MARTIN: Because it's nice.

Pause.

OLIVER: Where were you?

MARTIN: The truth?

OLIVER: Please, yeah. The truth. (*Beat.*) I know I haven't been too good at the truth but I need it now. I really do.

MARTIN: I needed time to think. (*Beat.*) About us. (*Beat.*) About me. (*Beat.*) I went and stayed with an old friend. From way back?

OLIVER: Did you sleep with her?

MARTIN: Did I sleep with her? (*Pause.*) Sorry. Yeah. But it didn't mean anything. Just a way of paying the rent. (*Pause.*) You wanted the truth.

OLIVER: It's all I ever wanted. (*Pause.*) And . . . Did you think?

MARTIN: Yeah.

OLIVER: And?

Beat.

MARTIN: What would you like me to say?

OLIVER: I don't know.

MARTIN: I mean . . .

Beat.

OLIVER: Are you going to need to go away and think any more?

MARTIN: I might.

OLIVER: Often?

Pause.

MARTIN: No. I don't think so.

OLIVER: Honest?

MARTIN: Honest.

OLIVER: Good. (*Pause.*) Martin. Come back. If you want to. I've changed. No more fussing. No more stupid ultimatums. Just us. Friends. Or more, if you want. (*Beat.*) What I'm saying is: I'll do anything to have you back. (*Beat.*) If you want sex . . .

MARTIN: Ollie . . . Let's just see what happens.

OLIVER: OK. (*Beat.*) What, you mean you're coming back?

MARTIN: Why not?

Beat.

OLIVER: It'll be different. I promise.

MARTIN: I believe you. (*They hug. MARTIN sings:*) 'Whoa-oh, these chains of love . . . (BRUCE *appears, wiping his hands on a cloth.*) . . . got a hold on me. Yeah.'

Blackout.

Scene Three

Monday evening, 9.30 p.m.
    LENNY *is sitting nervously at the table.*
ANGE *enters from the kitchen.*

ANGE: I'm busy. What d'you want?

Beat.

LENNY: What you doing?

ANGE: A barbeque. (*He looks away.*)
    Y'know, kebabs and things.

LENNY: I know what a barbeque is.

Pause.

ANGE: Well?

Beat.

LENNY: Y'know Tony? Landlord down
    the Duke? Yeah? (*She nods.*) I had a long
    chat with him the other night. (*Pause.*) I
    tried me dad, but . . . (*Pause.*) Tony says
    it ain't all my fault. Not all of it. We been
    stuck in that flat. Bloody rathole. So it
    ain't all my fault. But . . . (*Pause.*) He was
    telling me about his first wife.
    Apparently, she done a bunk when he hit
    her. (*Beat.*) Eight years ago. Still loves
    her, he says. (*Pause.*) Well, I was telling
    him about us and everything and he
    started having a right go at me. Yeah.
    (*Long pause.*) See, it's a question of
    respect. Gotta respect each other, ain't
    we? That's where we was going wrong. I
    didn't have no respect for you. (*Pause.*)
    And the thing is . . . I'd never thought
    about it.

ANGE: Lenny, don't go on. I'm not coming
    back.

Long pause.

LENNY: See, I got it all wrong. (*Pause.*)
    Tony says what we oughta do is: you get a
    job, if you can, start saving, and try and
    get a mortgage on a decent place. He
    reckons this is a good time to be buying
    your own house. Interest rates and that.

ANGE: What you talking about? Since
    when did you know anything about
    bloody interest rates?

LENNY: Since I talked to Tony.

ANGE: You have half an hour's chat with a
    bloody alcoholic and suddenly you know
    all about everything?

LENNY: He ain't alcoholic.

ANGE: Drinks like a fish.

LENNY: He helped me out. Advice and
    that.

ANGE: So go and live with *him*.

LENNY: I don't wanna live with him, I
    wanna live with you.

ANGE: Well, that's tough Lenny. I'm
    staying here. (*Pause.*) 'Cause, d'you
    know what? You're just an animal,
    Lenny. 'S all you are. I never knew till I
    came here. 'Cause you and your family
    and your mates, the lot of you, you're all
    just a pack of animals.

LENNY: That ain't fair.

ANGE: Bloody well is. And I'll tell you
    something else. I'd rather slit me wrists
    than come anywhere near you again.

Pause.

LENNY: Gimme another chance . . .

ANGE: I won't give you nothing. (WILL *is
    listening from the kitchen.*) Why should I?
    I'm starting again. New place. New
    people. (*Beat.*) Nice people. (*Beat.*) So
    go away, Lenny.

LENNY: It ain't fair.

ANGE: My heart bleeds.

LENNY: It ain't. I've tried to understand
    things. And you won't give me a bloody
    chance.

WILL *enters with a tray of cups.*

WILL: Sorry to break things up, but I'm
    just about to start cooking. So, if
    you're . . .

LENNY: Please, Ange . . .

WILL: Time to go, Lenny.

LENNY: I wasn't talking to you, cunt.

WILL: Careful. Or I might have to set my
    wife on you.

Beat.

ANGE: Time to go, Lenny.

Beat.

LENNY: You know what my dad said? He
    said you wouldn't have gone if I'd hit you
    where it didn't show. Said it was just
    'cause it was your face got marked.
    (*Pause.*) Look, you know where I am, if
    you . . . (*Beat.*) Fuck it. Fuck the lot of
    you.

He goes.

WILL: OK?

ANGE: Good riddance. (*Beat.*) I'll do those.

He kisses her. She pours wine into the cups. WILL runs his hand down her back. She turns.

Don't muck about.

WILL: This is serious.

She picks up the tray.

ANGE: I don't wanna spill this.

He runs his hands over her body. She can't move in case she spills the drinks.

Will . . .

WILL: You've got a . . . fantastic . . . body . . . (*He dissolves into laughter.*)

ANGE: Daft sod, you're drunk. (*He just laughs.*) Don't laugh at me.

WILL: I'm not . . .

ANGE: You are. Don't. I don't like it. (*He composes himself.*) 'S better.

He stares at her.

WILL: Hey, listen, don't forget . . .

ANGE: I dunno . . .

WILL: You promised.

ANGE: But, she might not . . .

WILL: Make her. You could make anybody do anything.

ANGE: Sure. And what about Andrea?

WILL: She rang. She's coming home alone.

Beat.

ANGE: I don't know if I can.

WILL: You can. (*He lifts a cup to her lips.*)

ANGE: I don't drink.

WILL: You do tonight.

Beat. She takes a swig. He makes her take a drag of the joint he's smoking.

OK?

ANGE: OK.

She starts to go as OLIVER, already fairly pissed, comes in. He takes a cup from the tray and she goes.

OLIVER: Give that woman a medal. (*Beat.*) Do you know, Will? Do you know what women are? What they really are? (*Beat.*) Apart from our sisters in the struggle, of course. Hmm?

WILL: You're either going to say something dreadfully silly or misogynist.

OLIVER: What? (*Beat.*) Me? I love women. Love them. The problem is, the problem is, Will . . . They don't love me.

WILL: Ah. Something dreadfully silly. That's a relief.

OLIVER: No, no, no, you don't understand. Non comprendo, old sausage. I mean, not *me*. I mean, all of us. Men. You. Me. All of us. (*Pause.*) Is that controversial, or what?

Beat.

WILL: Vague.

OLIVER: Oh, granted. You want chapter and verse?

WILL: No.

OLIVER: Why not?

WILL: You're pissed.

OLIVER: What the hell difference does that make? I'm being honest. I'm going to empty my soul.

WILL: You're going to bore me rigid, if you're not careful.

OLIVER: You can't take emotion, that's the trouble. Here I am, speaking from the heart, and all you want to do is shut me up. Well I won't be shut up. (*His voice rises to near tantrum level.*) This anal social life, this English, tight-arsed, clenched-buttock politeness. It should be . . . blown away. I won't shut up. I am a Russian. I am a Papua, New Guinea headhunter. I am alive.

MARTIN *has entered.*

MARTIN: Oh, shut up, Ollie.

Beat.

OLIVER: That's all they can say, isn't it. Oh, shut up. (*Beat.*) Shall I compare thee – oh, shut up. Tyger, Tyger, burning bright – put a sock in it, will you? We're British. Stiff upper lip. Arsehole like a vice. Emotion? The occasional fart. Love? One big shit. (*Pause.*) There's no poetry in life. No beauty.

The front door opens and MARK *enters.*

MARK: Yo.

OLIVER: This man looks like a fascist. Doesn't he? Tell me, are you a fascist? (MARK *is bemused.*) Come on, you're English, aren't you? You must be a fascist.

Beat.

MARK: What's this? Alternative cabaret?

OLIVER: Ha. A sense of humour. I like him. What's your name? I don't care if you are a fascist.

MARK: Go boil your bum.

WILL: His name's Mark.

OLIVER: Mark. Mark. I don't know if I like that. We might have to change it. (*Beat.*) I know. Vladimir. I'll call you Vladimir. OK, Vladimir? Or may I call you Vlad?

MARK: Don't be formal. Call me 'sir'.

OLIVER: Beneath his sarcasm is a soul of pure poetry. I can tell.

MARK *pats him on the face.*

MARK: When did they let *him* out?

WILL: Wait till the valium wears off.

MARTIN: Ollie. Let's grab some food.

OLIVER: Grab. Grab, grab, grab. Crab. Blab. Stab. Let's stab some food.

MARTIN: Whatever you say.

RONEE *enters.*

OLIVER (*to* RONEE): Why don't you love me?

He and MARTIN *go.*

RONEE: Oh, dear.

MARK: Where do you get your friends? Joke shop?

WILL (*aware of the joke*): Local Labour Party.

MARK: That's what I said.

WILL: For once, you might have a point.

RONEE: If tonight is going to consist of the poison dwarf embarrassing everyone in sight, I might just pass.

WILL: I think he's got it out of his system.

BRUCE *enters.*

Come and get some food.

RONEE: OK.

They go.

MARK: Hi. I'm Mark. I live here.

BRUCE: I'm Bruce. (*They shake.*)

MARK: You're not crackers like that other bloke, are you?

BRUCE: Who?

MARK: Short-arsed fella with the big mouth.

BRUCE: No.

Pause. BRUCE *pours himself a drink.*

MARK: Here, d'you hear the one about the two Irish queers? Patrick Fitzmaurice and Maurice Fitzpatrick?

Beat.

BRUCE: No . . . I didn't.

Beat.

MARK: I see.

BRUCE: What's a queer?

MARK: Eh?

BRUCE: What's a . . . queer?

Beat.

MARK: Well, you *have* led a sheltered life. A queer is a poof is a woofter.

BRUCE: Oh. Like . . . Pakis.

Beat.

MARK: Sort of.

BRUCE: And nig nogs.

Pause.

MARK: Except woofters are white.

ANGE *comes in with the tray and cups.*

ANGE: That stupid little git just knocked all the cups over, then collapsed on the rockery. Squashed all the flowers. Bloody nerd. (*She puts the cups out and starts pouring more wine.*)

MARK: Shouldn't you be wearing a pinny? And a mob cap?

ANGE: Tie a knot in it.

MARK: Could tie a sheep shank in mine. (*Beat.*) Here, seeing as you won't come upstairs to me, how about I come below stairs to you?

OLIVER *appears carrying a couple of squashed flowers.*

Here comes laughing boy again.

OLIVER: What have I done? Look. Murder. I've killed something of beauty.

MARK: Well, you know what they say. A thing of beauty is a boy forever.

OLIVER *goes over to him and puts his arm round his neck.*

OLIVER: Vlad. Oh, Vlad. Is this all that's left to us? Cruelty? Arbitrary killing and cruelty?

MARK: Yup.

OLIVER: It can't be. Where's hope?

MARK: In the bath with Faith and Charity.

ANGE (*enjoying it*): Don't.

OLIVER: Look what a precious jewel I've cast away . . .

MARK: Terrible.

OLIVER *absent-mindedly puts the flowers in his mouth and starts chewing them.*

ANGE: Oh, he's horrible.

She starts to go. As she passes OLIVER *he takes a cup. She goes.*

OLIVER: A toast. To flowers. Everywhere. May they forgive me? (*He drinks.*) Hey, listen . . . (*He starts to laugh.*) . . . Where have . . . Where have all the flowers gone? Eh? (*Beat.*) Squashed them all, haven't I? (*He laughs.*)

MARK: Yeah, nice one.

OLIVER: I like you, Vlad. Let's be friends. Hmm?

MARK: You smooth talking man.

RONEE *enters.*

OLIVER: I mean it. Let's be blood brothers. Cut our arms. Let the blood intermingle. What do you say?

MARK: Tell you what, I'll cut my arm if you cut your throat.

RONEE: If it's blood you're after, Will's just done some burgers.

MARK: Right. (*To* OLIVER:) Come on, smiler, let's find you some flowers to press.

OLIVER: They haunt me. Hollyhocks, geraniums, nasturtiums . . .

MARK: Pansies?

They leave.

RONEE: And hello, Bruce.

BRUCE: Hi.

RONEE: You know what this reminds me of?

BRUCE: What?

RONEE: The bad trips tent at the Isle of Wight festival. (*Beat.*) Actually, life sometimes reminds me . . . (*She waves her hand in the air and smiles.*) Found a flat, I hear.

BRUCE: That's right.

RONEE: Sharing it with a couple of leather queens . . . (BRUCE *looks worried.*) Come on, just a joke.

Pause.

BRUCE: One . . . is. The other isn't.

RONEE: Ah. (*Beat.*) And you've been a bit naughty, I also hear. (*He shrugs.*) Listen, can I ask you something?

BRUCE: Sure.

RONEE: This might sound odd . . . (*Beat.*) You're not married, or anything?

BRUCE: Not now.

Beat.

RONEE: Do you miss the security? Of a permanent relationship?

Beat.

BRUCE: I'm . . . not sure. Maybe. I'm not very . . . good with people. They don't stay very long. Sometimes . . . I want them to.

RONEE: Martin?

Beat.

BRUCE: Martin was just a fuck.

RONEE: Uh-huh. (*Beat.*) I might leave Will and live with Andrea. She wants me to. (*Beat.*) She's getting understandably pissed off. Having to share me, you see.

BRUCE: So's Will.

Beat.

RONEE: Poor old Will. When we first met,

y'know, I was a real wallflower. And he was something of a celebrity. Well, a big fish in a little pool.

Beat.

See, in the last nine, ten years, whatever it is, he hasn't changed. He's just sort of . . . got worse. (*Beat.*) He's like someone drowning. If you try to help, you just get dragged down. (*Beat.*) He tries. The men's group and what have you. But it's such an effort. I mean, you can see it. He's actually going against his nature.

BRUCE: But he's doing it for you.

Beat.

RONEE: Perhaps.

Pause.

BRUCE: His nature can change.

RONEE: I don't know about that.

BRUCE: He's changed in the time I've known him.

RONEE: How?

BRUCE: He . . . listens now. I mean . . . without offence . . . he's got things into perspective. Like . . .

RONEE: He's not such a big-headed bastard.

BRUCE: Yeah. No offence. (*Pause.*) You mean a lot. I think.

RONEE: Is that good or bad?

BRUCE: It's security. (*Beat.*) Yes, I do . . . miss it.

RONEE: So might I.

Pause.

BRUCE: I think you owe him a chance. (*Pause.*) Really.

WILL *enters.*

WILL: Hey, party poopers. (*He gets a drink.*) What's this? Illicit joint-smoking? The passing-out room? It's not that kind of party. I admit the paper cups may be somewhat reminiscent of a late sixties bring a bottle bash, but I like to think we've progressed.

Beat.

RONEE: I think you're enjoying yourself.

WILL: Darling, I'm having a ball.

RONEE: Good. (*She kisses him.*)

WILL: I'm now over the moon. Official. (ANGE *comes in.*) Hey, Bruce. Give us a hand with the fire, will you? It's a bugger to get re-started if it goes out.

BRUCE: I don't know . . . much about it . . .

WILL: Then learn, baby, learn.

They go. WILL *winks at* ANGE *as he goes.* RONEE *stretches out on the sofa.*

RONEE (*expansive*): Angela. Peel me a grape.

ANGE (*uptight*): Eh?

RONEE: Get me a glass of wine, angel. A glass. This is nineteen eighty-three and we're grown-ups now. (ANGE *pours a glass of wine, hands it to her and sits on the edge of the sofa.*) Ta. You know, I think I might have a cigarette. I think I dare. There's some on the table. (ANGE *gets them and sits.* RONEE *takes one out.* ANGE *lights it for her.*) Thanks love. (*She runs her hand down* ANGE*'s face and rests it on her shoulder.*) Well. Having a good time?

ANGE: Yeah.

RONEE: Good. Against all the odds, so am I. And I intend to have a better time.

ANGE, *misunderstanding, visibly relaxes.*

ANGE: It's all new to me.

RONEE: You'll get used to it. We're all a bit crazy. But then, who isn't?

ANGE: Right. (*Beat.*) Ronee. You ain't half been good to me. Letting me stay and everything. I really want to pay you back.

RONEE: You're your old self, that'll do for now.

ANGE: But I wish there was something . . . (*She leans down and gives her a friendly kiss, her hand now resting on* RONEE*'s shoulder.*) There.

RONEE: Where? (*She laughs.* ANGE *kisses her again.*)

ANGE: There. (*She laughs.*) There. (*She kisses her each time she says 'there'.*) There. There. There. (ANGE *starts running her hands over* RONEE*'s body.*)

RONEE: Ange . . . (*She breaks away and sits up.*) Break. Cool it. OK? (*Pause.* ANGE, *unsure what to do, slowly puts her arm round* RONEE*'s neck and tries to* *kiss her again.* RONEE *stands up.*) I don't know what you think you're doing, but whatever it is, don't.

ANGE: I was . . . (*She is completely shattered.*)

RONEE: I know what you was. Where the bloody hell'd you get the idea? . . . (*Beat.*) I mean, just because . . . (*Beat.*) Honestly, Ange . . .

ANGE: I'm sorry. I thought . . .

RONEE: What?

Pause.

Look, forget it. Don't feel you have to pay me back. You don't owe me anything. And you certainly don't want to complicate your life any more than it already is.

ANGE: That's not it.

RONEE: What?

ANGE: I wasn't trying to pay you back.

RONEE: What, just a sudden impulse, was it?

ANGE: No.

RONEE: Then what? (*Pause.*) Come on. (*Pause.*) What put the idea into your head . . . ? (*Beat.*) Oh no. (*Beat.*) Tell me Will had nothing to do with this. (*Beat.*) Ange. Tell me. Will. Tell me. (ANGE *nods her head.*) Oh, my Christ. I am so stupid. What a fool. What a soft bloody fool. (*She goes to the door.*) Will. (*Beat.*) Will!

WILL (*off*): What is it?

RONEE: Come here.

WILL (*off*): The fire'll go out.

RONEE: Too bloody right. (*Shouts:*) It's important.

WILL (*off*): OK.

RONEE *comes back into the room.*

ANGE: Ronee, I want to go home.

RONEE: No. Not yet.

WILL *enters.* ANGE *is sitting looking crushed.* WILL *is smiling. He slowly stops smiling.*

I told Ange that you and Lenny were very similar. I was wrong. You're worse than Lenny. Much worse. (*Beat.*) What you've done to her is certainly as bad as anything he did. (*Pause.*) That's not to mention

what you've done to me. Will, are you so insensitive, so feeble, that you had to do this?

Beat.

WILL: Er, yes?

Pause.

RONEE: Look at him, Ange. Look at him. There's your 'nice' man. There's your open, honest, charming man who can't get his mind past your tits. Whose idea of maturity is to screw everything in sight. (*Beat.*) Talking of which, did you? (*Beat.*) Did you two screw?

WILL: Yes, this morning . . .

RONEE: I don't want to know when, I don't want to see the pictures or . . . read the book or see the bloody film . . . (*Pause.*) Oh, why do I care? (*Beat.*) Will, did you seriously think that if you sent Ange in here to . . . That I would or could possibly go along with it? After everything I've told you? Did you?

WILL: Obviously.

RONEE: How?

WILL: Why should I change? I've done what you expected. You can't pretend to be disappointed.

RONEE: Don't you feel *anything* for anybody else?

Pause.

WILL: Contempt and lust. Those are my two strongest feelings.

RONEE: Why?!

Beat.

WILL: Because . . . I can't feel anything else. I can't love anybody. I can't even bring myself to like very many people. (*Beat.*) I keep thinking back to ten years ago, when people *did* things. Nobody was expected to do the 'right' thing. We just did them, right or wrong, good or bad, nasty or nice. (*Beat.*) Thing is, I think I preferred them wrong, bad and nasty. Is that a crime?

RONEE: It hurts people.

WILL: So what? (*Pause.*) The problem with you is, you still want love. After everything, after all the disillusion, the naked facts of life, the ugliness, the pointlessness, the kicks in the teeth, the bad scenes in bed, the downright bloody failure . . . You . . . still want love. Well, where is it? Andrea? She got it? Is Andrea a mystical receptacle of all that's good and fair in life? Is she?

RONEE: No. She's another human being who wants love. Who wants me.

WILL: Then you deserve each other.

RONEE: Yes! (*Pause.*) Nobody deserves you. Nobody who ever smiled or had a simple thought without wanting to soil somebody else deserves you. Live in the dirt. There are plenty of others there like you. But don't ever expect to find me down there again. I'm going to live knowing that I don't need to cut people to prove they're flesh and blood. Knowing that I don't need to smear their faces in shit to prove that it exists. Knowing, most of all, that I don't need to carve my name on their face to prove that *I* exist.

Beat. Enter OLIVER.

WILL: Well, climb every mountain.

RONEE *goes.* OLIVER *sings, loudly:*

OLIVER: Ford every stream. Follow every rainbow. *Till you find your dream*!! I have always wanted . . . to perform . . . cunnilingus . . . on Julie Andrews! I admit it.

WILL: And I have always had a secret desire to roger Judith Chalmers.

OLIVER: Anna Ford.

WILL: Valerie Singleton.

OLIVER: The Queen.

WILL: The world.

MARK *comes in, followed by* MARTIN *and* BRUCE, *who leans in the doorway, watching.*

Mark here, has no secret desire whatsoever. Do you, Mark? Because little Mark's desires are always well out in front where they ought to be.

OLIVER: Vladimir, me old pal, is this right?

MARK: I don't know what you're on about.

OLIVER: We're talking about desire. The turgid electricity in the loins. The dark, insatiable fire in the belly. Fucking.

MARK: I dunno.

OLIVER: Well, that's not a very intelligent remark, is it for chrissakes? I expect better of you, Vlad.

MARTIN: Ollie, do us a favour.

OLIVER: Certainly. What had you in mind?

MARTIN: Keep it down.

OLIVER: Keep it down? I have trouble keeping it up. (*Liberal helpings of drink are being poured.*) The one-minute wonder, they used to call me. Oh, yes. Inoutinoutinout? In, mate. That was my lot. Thank you for coming, do call again.

MARK: Here, this bloke, right. He's just got out of the nick. Been in for thirty years. And he thinks, 'Christ do I need a fuck.' So he goes off, right, and finds this scabby old whore, throws it on the bed and gives it the shagging of its life. When he's finished, he says, 'That was good. Just one thing, though.' 'What's that?' she says. 'Why was it that every time I give it some thrust, your toes turned up?' 'Next time,' she says, 'remember to take my tights off.' (MARK, OLLIE *and* WILL *laugh.* MARTIN *looks embarrassed.* BRUCE *just stares.*)

OLIVER: Hey, you should join our group. We could do with a few laughs.

MARTIN: Ollie, let's go home.

OLIVER: And rut like healthy stags.

MARTIN: Let's just go home.

OLIVER: I . . . am . . . enjoying myself. I am letting it all hang out.

MARTIN: Fab.

Pause.

OLIVER (*slurring*): What is it? What's all this? . . . Killjoys . . . Why can't I have fun, for once? Just for once in my life, why can't I fart in church?

MARTIN: Because it's stupid.

OLIVER: How dare you?! You dare to call me stupid?! Why, I've got more brains in my big toe than you've got in your entire body. I was a socialist when you were in nappies. I'm still a better socialist than you.

MARTIN: What's that got to . . .

OLIVER: Everything. I am a socialist. I don't kowtow to the ruling class.

MARTIN: What are you talking about?

OLIVER: Socialism's about truth and love and fucking. It's blood and sperm. What do Tories know about fucking? Nothing.

(*In a tantrum:*) I've fucked my way around the world. There's nothing you can tell me. I've fucked socialists, fascists, pigs, my mother, myself. So I know what I'm talking about. *All right*?!

MARTIN: If you say so.

OLIVER: I do say so! And don't contradict me. (*He hurls his drink in* MARTIN's *face.*)

MARTIN: For God's sake, Ollie . . .

OLIVER: God? How the fuck did he get into this? I've fucked god. (*He pours whatever he can lay his hands on over* MARTIN's *head.*) God is a Nazi. And I don't have anything to do with Nazis. I shit on them. I fuck them. You're a Nazi. You're an anti-semite. Don't tell me you're not, because . . . (*He bawls into his face.*) *I know you bloody are!* (*Pause.*) I'm sorry, but you deserved that.

Pause.

MARTIN: It wasn't a woman. It was Bruce.

He goes.

OLIVER (*advancing on* BRUCE): Ha. So. (*Beat. He stops.*) What?

Pause. He suddenly lunges at BRUCE, *attempting to throw a punch.* BRUCE *clocks it and knees him in the stomach. He falls to the ground out of breath and hurt.*

BRUCE: I won't be . . . coming to the group any more. I don't think I . . . need it.

He goes.

MARK: Often like this, is it? (*He picks up* OLIVER *and dumps him on the sofa.*)

WILL: Better, usually.

MARK: Don't know what I've been missing.

OLIVER (*doubled up*): Christ, what happened?

WILL: Martin went.

OLIVER: Where?

WILL: How the fuck should I know?

OLIVER: Vlad, Vlad, come and live with me.

MARK: Sure thing.

RONEE *enters.*

WILL: Ah. Goodnight, sweet lady.

RONEE: Yeah. Ange, get your case. You're coming with me.

ANGE *goes upstairs.*

WILL: Ronee . . .

RONEE: Don't, Will. You know where you're going. See it through. You might as well. It's all you've got.

WILL: It is now.

Beat.

RONEE: I'll pick my stuff up tomorrow. And I'll see my solicitor.

WILL: What's it going to be? Mental cruelty?

RONEE: I hadn't thought about it. But yeah, I think mental cruelty would do very nicely.

WILL: Y'know, deep down, deep inside somewhere . . . I hate you. I think I always have.

RONEE: You poor, dried up little man. (*Beat.*) I used to love you.

ANGE *reappears.*

WILL: Yeah. Funny, isn't it?

RONEE: Bloody hilarious . . .

She and ANGE *go.*

MARK: Don't forget to leave that window open . . . (*Beat.*) You must be mad. What I wouldn't have done for a piece of your wife.

WILL: What *I* wouldn't have done . . .

Beat.

MARK: Why don't we drop the laughing gnome off and hit the town? Maybe pick up some crumpet.

WILL: I dunno . . .

MARK: Listen. We've never been out for a drink together, you and me. Let's go and get ratarsed, find some dirty slags and have a bachelor night. Eh?

Beat.

WILL: Be just like old times. (*Pause.*) No. Not tonight, Josephine.

OLIVER (*holding up a flower*): Look what I did. Why did I do that?

MARK: 'Cause you're a prick.

OLIVER: No, no, no, I've got a prick.

MARK: I call them as I see them.

He nods to WILL *and goes.* WILL *finishes his glass and goes to* OLIVER, *who is asleep.* WILL *sighs and goes to the stereo. He switches it on. The tape plays.*

OLIVER: I need help.

MARTIN: Ollie, don't make it so hard on yourself.

OLIVER: I can't help it. (*Beat.*) I'm sorry everyone, I'm talking too much. I'm sorry. I'll give someone else a chance.

WILL: It's OK. It's not right to keep it bottled up, Ollie. It's not honest. (*Beat.*) No, I really think we're getting somewhere here. Let's keep going.

End.

HARD FEELINGS

Hard Feelings was first seen at the Oxford Playhouse on 5 November, 1982, with the following cast:

VIVIENNE, *25. An unpredictable, slightly matronly woman, prone to nervousness and sudden changes of mood. Not conventionally attractive, not totally unattractive either. She is a university graduate, temporarily out of work.*	Frances Barber
JANE, *24. A law student studying for Part Twos at a London college. She has Jewish dark good looks. She is quite timid, but fierce and stubborn when cornered.*	Jenifer Landor
ANNIE, *25. A part-time model and artist. She is fashionably beautiful. She is acid and devious, though easily put off.*	Diana Katis
RUSTY, *24. He is 'hip' or 'cool'. Has an exaggerated sense of style, and dresses in New Romantic fashion. He is studiedly casual.*	Ian Reddington
BAZ, *24. He is the national organiser of the UK Frisbee Association. A Northerner, he is short and easy going, though assertive when he wants to be.*	Chris Jury
TONE, *27. Jane's boyfriend. He is educated working-class, working as a freelance contributor to political papers and magazines. He is outspoken and aggressive.*	Stephen Tiller

Directed by Mike Bradwell
Designed by Geoff Rose
Lighting by Raymond Cross
Sound by Jan Bevis Hughes

This production was subsequently seen at the Bush Theatre, London on 3 February 1983.

The play is set in a newly gentrified house in Brixton. The set is the living-room and kitchen area, which is actually part of the living-room, separated by a counter. The action begins in April 1981.

ACT ONE

Scene One

RUSTY *and* ANNIE *are asleep on the sofa-bed, under a sleeping bag. It is 11 a.m. Sunday morning. The room is very messy; empty beer cans, wine bottles, clothes all over the place.* TONE *enters, goes to the fridge, takes out a pint of milk and swigs. He peers round the room and sees* RUSTY *and* ANNIE. *He walks across the room, watching them, and picks up a pack of cigarettes. He opens it; it's empty.*

TONE: Ah.

He crushes the empty packet and starts to go, throwing the packet over his shoulder. BAZ *enters wearing a dressing-gown and a Sony Walkman, grooving to the music. He is taking a cigarette out of a packet.* TONE *takes the cigarette.*

Ta.

He goes out. BAZ *takes out another cigarette and lights it. Door slams off.* BAZ *walks across to the window, singing along with the tape.*

BAZ: Goin' back to my roots . . .

He peers through the venetian blinds. RUSTY *groans.* BAZ *goes out.*

RUSTY: Whaaa . . . ?

He puts his head back down. Pause. JANE *enters and puts the kettle on. She thinks about putting the light on, hesitates, shrugs and puts it on. She puts cornflakes in two bowls and coffee in two cups.* RUSTY *groans and pulls the sleeping bag over his head.*

JANE: Sorry. I only live here.

She picks up the bowls and starts to go off. VIV *enters.*

Hi.

VIV: Hi. (*Beat.*) How do you do it?

JANE: Do what?

VIV: Look so great first thing in the morning?

JANE (*slightly embarrassed*): Dunno. Clean living, I s'pose.

VIV: Yeah, probably.

JANE *goes off.* VIV *stands for a moment, then opens the blinds and puts on the table-lamps.*

Rise and shine. (*She tousles* ANNIE's *hair.*) C'mon. (ANNIE *wakes and looks around.*)

ANNIE: Oh.

VIV: Hi.

ANNIE: Hi.

VIV: Coffee?

ANNIE *nods.*

ANNIE: Whassa time?

VIV: Nearly eleven?

ANNIE *counts on her fingers.*

ANNIE: That's only five hours. (*She feels under her eyes.*) I'll get bags. What a life. (*She nudges* RUSTY.) C'mon, slob, wake up. (*He stirs.*) Wake up. (*She pushes him. He groans and puts his head in his hands.*)

RUSTY: Fuck. Oh . . . Fuck. (*He sits up, putting his foot in an ashtray.*) Shit!

ANNIE: This man has an English degree.

VIV: Don't we all?

ANNIE: Hundred words a minute, darling, that's all I've got. Well, that and my sublime good looks.

RUSTY: Christ, this room looks like I feel.

ANNIE: Yeah, but the room we can straighten up.

RUSTY: I'll have to stop enjoying myself so often. It's killing me. (*He starts to roll a joint.*)

VIV: Get up, will you? I want to hoover.

RUSTY: Leave it. Live fast, die young, right? Bugger the mess.

VIV: Bugger you. (*She brings their coffees.*)

RUSTY: What's the scam, then?

ANNIE: We could go and see if Nigel's still alive.

VIV: No, I want to go to Camden Lock, buy some clothes.

ANNIE: Aren't we s'posed to be having lunch at Nigel's?

VIV: We can take him to Routiers.

ANNIE: Or he could take us.

VIV *picks up the phone and dials.*

RUSTY: Why don't we just meet Nigel at the Elgin?

ANNIE: 'Cause it's full of middle-aged wogs.

RUSTY: Tut, tut.

ANNIE: Still trendy to like wogs, is it?

RUSTY: Trendy? *De rigeur,* darling. James Brown is muh maaan.

ANNIE: Well, it's one fad I'm not falling for.

RUSTY: It'll be the first.

VIV (*into the phone*): Nigel? It's me. Vivienne. D'you get home all right last night? (*Pause.*) How much? (*Pause.*) Are you up yet? (*Pause.*) OK. So it's plan B.

RUSTY: The Elgin.

VIV: Camden Lock, lunch at Routiers.

RUSTY: The Elgin.

VIV: And a drink at the Elgin. OK?

ANNIE: Oh, for God's sake.

RUSTY: Don't pout.

ANNIE: It's not you who gets your bum groped.

RUSTY: Wanna bet?

VIV (*into the phone*): OK. See you in about half an hour. (*Pause.*) Yeah. See you. (*She puts the phone down and shouts:*) Baz? You up yet? (*Pause.*) Baz? (BAZ *enters, singing along to the tape.*)

He's up. (*She lifts his headphones.*) Camden Lock, Routiers. OK?

He nods and goes. He comes back.

BAZ: I thought we were having lunch at Nigel's.

VIV *shakes her head. He goes.*

RUSTY: Time I abluted. (*He gets up and picks up his clothes.*)

ANNIE: Time you aborted.

VIV: Knock it off, you two. You've only just woken up.

RUSTY: We can row in our sleep.

He goes.

ANNIE: Too right.

VIV: You gonna keep this up all day?

ANNIE: Sorry. (*Pause.*) I think Rusty gets off on crashing on your sofa. I woke up and he was still at it. Must think you're watching through the keyhole.

VIV: I've got better things to do.

ANNIE: You'll wear the batteries out. (*Pause.*) I tell you. Viv, Rusty gets on my tits. Literally. (*She shouts:*) And don't take all the hot water, slob!

VIV: None to take. It was all gone when I got up. 'Someone' had used it all.

ANNIE: Any prizes for guessing who?

VIV *gives a mirthless smile.* RUSTY *enters.*

RUSTY: Viv, how can I shave in cold water?

VIV: Take the kettle.

He does.

RUSTY: Christ, get the tin bath out.

He goes.

ANNIE: She does it on purpose. She must do. (*Pause.*) I couldn't put up with it.

VIV: Well . . .

Pause.

ANNIE: Is she likely to move in with her new man?

VIV: Dunno.

ANNIE: If she does, remember I'm looking for somewhere.

VIV: 'Course. (*Pause.*) Don't think she will, though.

ANNIE: But if she does . . .

VIV: I won't forget. (*She kisses* ANNIE *on top of her head.*)

JANE *enters. She looks for the kettle.*

JANE: What happened to the kettle?

VIV: Rusty took it. He's shaving.

ANNIE: There was no hot water.

Pause.

JANE: It's just . . . I put it on for coffee.

VIV: *You* put it on? Sorry, I've used your cups as well.

JANE: Doesn't matter.

VIV: I'll get you some more.

JANE *goes off.*

ANNIE: Whose bloody kettle is it?

VIV: Annie . . .

ANNIE: Pain in the arse.

VIV: She'll hear you.

ANNIE: I should worry.

JANE *enters with the kettle.*

VIV: Let me do it. (*She takes the kettle.*)

ANNIE: Anybody got any aspirins?

VIV: They're on the shelf.

ANNIE: Oh. (*Pause.*) Jane, you couldn't . . . ?

JANE: Sorry, yeah. (*She gets the aspirins and gives them to* ANNIE.) They're not very good for you, y'know.

ANNIE: Is that right?

JANE: Yeah. They make your stomach bleed.

ANNIE: Oh. I'll remember that. (*She swallows them.*)

BAZ *enters.*

BAZ: Give us a break, girls. Not all three at once, eh?

ANNIE: Hark at the virgin prince. (*Pause.*)

BAZ (*tries again*): Sleep well, happy campers?

ANNIE: What d'you think? (*Pause.*)

JANE: What was Rusty's group like last night?

ANNIE: Band, dear, band.

VIV: They were really good.

BAZ: If you've never seen Kraftwerk. All style, no content, you ask me.

ANNIE: We didn't.

BAZ: I mean, they just stand there poking at their Stylaphones. They don't *do* anything.

ANNIE: What d'you want them to do? Get on down and boogie?

BAZ: It beats watching rigor mortis set in.

ANNIE: It's supposed to be conceptual, dummy.

BAZ: Oh, it was. Very.

VIV: D'you want to go and get the papers, Baz?

JANE: It's OK. Tone's gone.

ANNIE: Ah. Tone. I get to meet him at last. What's he like?

VIV: Not your type.

ANNIE: And what, exactly, is my type?

BAZ: Conceptual rigor mortis.

ANNIE: He's my affliction, not my type.

BAZ: Let's just say Tone doesn't wax his legs or use nail varnish.

ANNIE: Oh, God. Don't tell me he's dirty-fingernail-and-bomber-jacket brigade. I can see it now: he drops his aitches, drinks Carlsberg Special Brew – from the can – is heavily into Bob Marley and wants to smash the Tory government.

BAZ: Sounds like a nice boy.

ANNIE: If you like that kind of thing.

JANE: People aren't kinds of things. They're people.

ANNIE: Not in my experience.

JANE: I'm sure.

ANNIE: No, dear. In my experience, people play it strictly by the book. The handbook of social conditioning, and all that.

BAZ: Depends how you look at it.

ANNIE: Sorry?

BAZ: I said . . . depends how you look at it.

Pause.

ANNIE: Well, Baz. You really have cornered the market in stupid comments, haven't you?

BAZ: Bollocks.

ANNIE: Oh, scathing.

Pause.

VIV: Can I have your rent cheques today? And there's an electric bill to pay.

JANE: How much?

VIV: Thirty-five each.

BAZ: What?

VIV: It's right. They checked it.

BAZ: Bloody hell. Rusty's gonna have to start buying his own.

JANE: Can I give it to you tomorrow? I'll have to get it off my mum.

VIV: I wanted to pay them tomorrow.

JANE: If I give you a cheque now, it might bounce.

VIV: Me, too, that's the trouble.

BAZ: Pay it on Tuesday.

VIV: I want to do it tomorrow, OK?

JANE: How about if I give you the rent today and the electric tomorrow?

Beat.

VIV: Yeah, that'll be all right.

JANE: I'll get my cheque book.

VIV: Don't worry. Do it later.

JANE: Might as well do it now.

She goes off.

ANNIE: Like getting blood out of a stone. (*She rubs her nose.*) If you know what I mean.

BAZ: I should leave those sort of comments in the playground.

ANNIE: Hmm? Sorry, don't follow.

BAZ (*to* VIV): I'll give you mine later.

VIV: No hurry. Can't pay it in till tomorrow, anyway.

BAZ: What's all the fuss about, then?

VIV: I just want to make sure I get it, that's all.

Door slams off stage.

BAZ: 'Course, you'll get it.

ANNIE: She doesn't mean yours, silly.

BAZ: Fucking hell.

TONE *enters with* The Observer *and* Sunday Times.

TONE: Mornin' all.

ANNIE: Well hello, Tone.

TONE: Hello.

ANNIE: I'm Annie. (*She holds out her hand.*)

TONE: Yeah, I guessed. (*He shakes her hand. She stares at his fingernails.*) It's a hand.

ANNIE: I know. With fingernails.

TONE: Yeah. I got a full set. Wanna see me teeth?

ANNIE: It's a bit early for me.

TONE: Some other time.

ANNIE: Who knows?

JANE *enters and hands* VIV *a cheque.*

VIV: Thanks.

JANE (*to* TONE): Coffee?

TONE: Ta.

VIV *and* BAZ *both take bits of the papers and sit and read at the table.* TONE, *looking slightly annoyed, takes a bit of the paper.*

ANNIE: Well. This is cosy. (*Pause.*) I said . . .

BAZ: Shut up, woman, I'm trying to read.

ANNIE: Keep trying. You'll get the hang of it. (*Pause.*) Newspapers are so boring.

BAZ: Blah blah blah.

Pause. JANE *gives* TONE *his coffee.*

ANNIE: Look at you. Bunch o' stiffs. What's so interesting about bloody papers anyway?

TONE: It's called information.

ANNIE: About what?

TONE: Oh, this an' that.

VIV: And 'Peanuts'.

Pause.

ANNIE: Sorry?

VIV: 'Peanuts'. In the magazine. (*She holds it up.*)

ANNIE: Oh, 'Peanuts'. Well, that changes everything. Sling it over. Let me read and learn. (*Pause.*) 'Peanuts'. Christ.

VIV: You gonna be like this all day?

ANNIE: Who knows? I have a feeling it could be one of those days. I mean, you know how it is when you wake up in the morning and get out the wrong side of the futon.

She stands, naked, picks up her clothes and goes off.

TONE: She often do that?

VIV: What?

TONE: Stumble around wi' nothin' on.

VIV: I didn't notice.

TONE: I did.

JANE: It's a bit . . .

VIV: What?

JANE: Unnecessary.

BAZ: Only does it to be noticed.

JANE: It worked.

BAZ: It's yer sheltered upbringing, lass.

TONE: Naah. We've all seen Woodstock, maaan.

Pause. VIV gets up and goes off.

BAZ: Ah. Baz's first law. Never criticise Viv's pals. It'll only end in tears. (*Pause.*) Baz's second law. Keep *stumm* and keep your head down. (TONE *glowers at him.*) I think I just broke that one.

TONE (*arch*): You must let me have a copy of the rules. I'd so hate to make a gaffe.

BAZ: They're highly strung round here. You have to play it by ear.

TONE: You know me. Only open me mouth to change feet.

BAZ: No good playing dumb. Can't have two of us doing that.

TONE: How about if I maintain a dignified silence?

BAZ: That's just dumb with an English degree.

TONE: Which would seem to be the prevailing human condition round here.

JANE: So don't come round then.

Pause.

TONE: Joke? (*Pause.*) No? (*Pause.*) For fuck's sake, darlin' . . .

JANE: Oh, shut up.

BAZ: Time for Baz's second law.

TONE: You should know.

VIV (*off*): Hurry up, you two. (*She comes on.*) And you, Baz.

BAZ: I'm ready.

Pause. She puts up the futon; JANE helps.

VIV: Are you two staying in all day?

JANE: Probably.

VIV: Don't forget to double lock the door if you go out. (*Pause.*) I'll feel a lot happier when the burglar alarm's put in.

TONE: Burglar alarm?

VIV: Yeah. What's wrong with that?

TONE: Nothin'. I s'pose.

VIV: The number of break-ins you get round here's incredible.

TONE: Yeah? I don't find it very hard to believe.

VIV: You know what I mean.

TONE: Oh, yeah. I know what you mean.

Pause.

VIV: Nothing wrong with wanting to protect your own property, y'know.

TONE: Never said there was.

VIV: I've got every right to live here.

TONE: Course. you've got a nice house, an' you wanna keep it that way, I can understand that.

VIV: Thank you very much.

TONE: 'S OK.

VIV: I bet you'd do the same.

TONE: I might.

VIV: Well, then.

TONE: Well, then.

Pause. RUSTY enters. He looks stunning, fully done up in New Romantic gear.

RUSTY: I'm ready for the world. Is the world ready for me?

BAZ: You're never coming out like that.

RUSTY: And why not?

BAZ: Eee lad, I don't know where we went wrong. It's enough to make you throw your bollocks at the clock.

RUSTY: London's swinging again. I intend to swing with it.

BAZ: It's OK on stage, but . . .

RUSTY: But in the real world it's all fade to grey, right? Let's all do the conformity dance, right? No chance. This is me. If people don't like it . . .

TONE: Let them eat cake.

RUSTY: Right. (*Pause. He is not amused.*) Ha ha. (*Pause.*) Who is this person?

BAZ: This is Tone.

RUSTY: Yes it is, isn't it.

TONE: 'Ullo.

RUSTY *gives a mirthless smile.*

JANE: I really like your trousers.

RUSTY: Jodphurs, darling. Jodphurs.

BAZ: I give up.

RUSTY: Right. Full stop.

ANNIE *pops her head round the door.*

ANNIE: Viv. Borrow a T-shirt?

VIV: Yeah.

ANNIE: Where are they?

VIV: I'll show you.

She goes off.

TONE: Does it really bother you that much?

RUSTY: Does what really bother me that much?

TONE: Clothes. What people think.

RUSTY: It bothers people. It doesn't bother me.

TONE: Proper little threat to society, aren't we?

BAZ (*mock professor*): Ze vay I see it, Rusty is reacting against ze industrial drabness of contemporary Britain by making his stand as ze individual against ze crowd; by asserting his free spirit against ze dreaded collective vill. (*Beat.*) And ziz he does by going to clubs, vere two hundred uzzer free spirits stand around in identical clothes looking at each uzzer.

RUSTY: Piss off back to Bradford, Baz.

BAZ: Sheffield.

RUSTY: Look, Baz, baby, I don't make jokes about what a wimp you are, or about the fact that your jacket's at least two sizes too big for you. So stay off my back and I'll stay off yours, OK?

BAZ: Touch-ee.

RUSTY: I just don't need the hassle, right?

BAZ: Whatever you say. (*He flashes a peace sign.*)

RUSTY: Look, I'll let you off, you do one thing for me.

BAZ: How much?

RUSTY: A fiver.

BAZ: You must be joking. I'm skint.

RUSTY: Well, so am I. Obviously.

BAZ: What about your dole?

RUSTY: In case you hadn't noticed, Baz, the bastards are on a work to rule. I haven't had a giro for two weeks. So come on.

BAZ: I haven't got a fiver to lend you.

RUSTY: Fucking hell. (*Pause.*) Jane? Till the end of the week? A measly fiver?

JANE: I'll have to have it back.

RUSTY: What d'you think I'm gonna do? Emigrate with it?

JANE: End of the week?

RUSTY: Yeah.

Beat.

JANE: OK.

RUSTY: You're an angel. (*To* BAZ:) And you're a shit.

TONE (*to* JANE): An' you bin done.

JANE (*giving* RUSTY *a fiver*): Just don't forget.

RUSTY: Scout's honour. (*He gives her a peck on the cheek as* ANNIE *comes back in.*)

ANNIE: Well. Can anyone join in?

RUSTY: Just sealing a financial transaction.

ANNIE: Thought there must be a reason. Spontaneous demonstrations of affection not being exactly your thing.

RUSTY: I can be nice when I want to be.

ANNIE: Yeah. Calculating sod.

VIV *enters.*

VIV: We ready then?

BAZ: I've been ready for half an hour.

VIV: We'll clean up when we get back.

JANE: I'll do it. Don't worry.

VIV: Don't be silly. It's our mess. Right. See you later.

JANE: Bye.

ANNIE: Enjoy the papers, Tone.

TONE: I intend to.

They go. As the front door slams, JANE *and* TONE *both exhale loudly.*

Jesus Christ.

JANE: You said it.

TONE: What'd you give that creep a fiver for?

JANE: Could hardly refuse, could I?

TONE: Last you'll see of it.

JANE: Better bloody not be.

TONE: Look on the bright side. I think I'd quite enjoy wringing his neck if he don't cough up. (*Pause.*) C'mere. (*She sits on his lap. They kiss.*) 'Ow d'you get shacked up wi' this nest o' vipers, anyway?

JANE: They're my friends.

TONE: Unlucky, son.

Pause.

JANE: Wanna go back to bed?

TONE: What a good idea.

They turn to the door. The phone rings. She answers it.

Hello? (*Pause.*) Yeah. (*To* TONE:) It's for you. Someone called Lloyd.

TONE: Ah. Do us a drink, will you? (*He takes the phone.*) Hi, Lloyd. (*Pause.*) Hang on, hang on, I can't hear you, you're talkin' too fast. (*Pause.*) 'Old it a minute. (*He gets his notebook and writes.*) Right. (*Pause.*) Who knifed him? (*Pause.*) Uh huh. How old is he? (*Pause.*) I'm just trying to get a story. (*Pause.*) How many? (*Pause.*) Any ol' bill get hurt? (*Pause. He smiles.*) I'd like to've seen that. (*Pause.*) What, SPG? (*Pause.*) So, what's the score now? (*Pause.*) You reckon? (*Pause.*) OK. Where are you? (*Pause.*) The Railway. Yeah, I know it. I'll be all right, will I? (*Pause.*) Is it worth comin' down now? (*Pause.*) I can do. (*Pause.*) OK. Say one o'clock outside the Railway. (*Beat.*) Hey listen, man, put a bleedin' film in your camera this time, will you? (*Pause. He laughs.*) Yeah, up yours an' all. One o'clock. See you. (*He puts the phone down and looks in the A to Z.*)

JANE: What's happened?

He raises his hand.

TONE (*to himself*): Bingo. (*He shuts the book.*)

JANE: Tone?

TONE: Some black kid gets himself knifed. The ol' bill are givin' 'im first aid. Crowd gathers. Think he's gettin' roughed up. They go ape-shit. Turn the car over, the lot.

JANE: My God, where?

TONE (*he points*): About four 'undred yards . . . that way.

Pause.

JANE: So, are you going out?

TONE: Not yet.

JANE: Is it safe?

TONE: Dunno. (*Pause.*) 'S OK. Any trouble, I'll just flash me NUJ card. (*Pause.*) Wanna drink?

She starts tidying up.

What you doin'?

JANE: Cleaning up.

TONE: What for?

JANE: Because it's a mess.

TONE: It's their mess. Viv said so. Let them clean it up.

JANE: She knows I'll do it.

TONE: So don't.

JANE: I've got to. There'll only be a broody silence if I don't.

TONE: So? Let her brood.

JANE: It's not worth it. (*She tidies up.*)

TONE: You oughta give this place a name. Little plaque on the front gate. Something nice an' cosy, to go with the burglar alarm. 'The Pressure Cooker.' How about that? Very domestic. Or p'raps, 'Dunthinkin'.

JANE: Stop it.

Pause.

TONE: I thought we was goin' back to bed.

JANE: I thought you were going out.

TONE: Not yet.

JANE: Don't let me stop you.

TONE: I won't. (*Pause.*) Fuckin' burglar

alarm . . . (*Pause.*) Look, I'm not meetin'
Lloyd for an hour an' a half . . . (*He puts
his arms round her.*) We could have a
bath.

JANE: I've had one.

TONE: Have another one.

JANE: If you don't think Lloyd'll mind.

TONE: You got work to do, ain't you? So.
I'll be outa your way.

JANE: But, I don't want you out of my way.

TONE: Can't spend your whole life in bed.

JANE: Can try. (*They kiss.*) Water should
be hot.

TONE: Makes two of us. C'mon then.

JANE: Wait. (*She quickly tidies the
counter.*)

TONE: Leave it. (*She does and starts to go.
As he goes:*) This is Tony March. News at
Ten. South London. (*He laughs and
goes.*)

Fade.

Scene Two

Six forty-five that evening. TONE *is sitting
very still with a look of mild horror on his
face, watching Songs of Praise on the TV. A
hymn is playing very loud. He has a pile of
papers and notes on his lap. He finishes his
drink and stands, rather wobbly. He pours
the last of the vodka and goes and looks out
the window. He then turns the TV down,
picks up the phone and dials.*

TONE: Lloyd? Tone. How'd the pictures
come out? (*Pause.*) Great. (*Pause.*)
Yeah, I'm writin' it up now. I don't wanna
make it too . . . sorta final, y'know.
(*Pause. He laughs.*) Yeah. (*He gives a
short whoop of joy.*) Look, why don't you
meet me in the boozer over the road?
(*Pause.*) I dunno. The Lamb an'
somethin' or other. Lamb an' Goose, I
dunno. (*Pause.*) 'Bout 'alf an hour.
(*Pause.*) Right. Yeah, I'm 'alf outa me
tree now. (*He's about to put the phone
down.*) Eh? (*Pause.*) Never. (*Pause.*)
Swamp as in . . . ? (*Pause.*) Boy, oh boy.
(*Pause.*) OK. See you. (*He puts the phone
down.*) Come on, God, strut that funky
stuff. (*He turns the TV up. A door slams
off stage.*) Oh, oh.

He sits. VIV *enters with her shopping.*

VIV: Hi. (*He waves. She puts her shopping
down and pours a scotch.*)

TONE (*agonised*): Enough. (*He turns the
TV off. She stares at him.*) You
weren't . . ?

VIV: No. Just surprised you were.

TONE: Anti-torture training. Seein' 'ow
long I could stand it. Bit of a failure,
really. The SAS'd only 'ave to come in
singing 'Abide wiv Me' an' I'd be putty in
their 'ands. (*Beat.*) Hymns. Oughta be
kept in their proper place. Church.
Christmas. Fuck. Christmas. My ol'
mum, y'know – godless ol' bugger three
'undred an' sixty four days o' the year.
Then Christmas comes along an' wallop.
Feudal 'ysteria. I say to 'er, 'Mum, what
are you doin'?' Y'know, she's singing
along wi' the goons on the box. She says,
'Sod off. Ain't doin' you no 'arm.' No
'arm in civilised people prattin' about
celebratin' the invisible? 'S all a bit
Freudian, you ask me. 'Ands an' buttocks
clenched in the kneelin' position, 'avin' a
rabbit wi' the almighty invisible one . . .
Belongs in the Karma Sutra. (*Pause.*)
What was I sayin'? (*Beat.*) Yeah, Christ,
we all 'ave a good laugh at the Druids on
Salisbury Plain every summer, don't we?
An' that bloke, what's 'is name, outa
Coronation Street, 'e's one. (*Beat.*)
Druid. Ken Barlow. Prat. (*Beat.*) But
'ave a good look at St Paul's. What is it?
I'll tell you. Stonehenge built by
unionised labour. Thass what St Paul's is.
(*Beat.*) No 'arm? As far as its 'arm value
goes, I'd stick it on a par wi' the stock
exchange, Soviet Communism and the
MacDonald's hamburger. (*Pause.*)
Where'd I start on this?

VIV: Christmas, I think.

TONE: Christmas? I 'ate Christmas. An'
churches. An' Christians. I mean, they
seem to think that 'cause they left their
brains at the door on the way in, we gotta
do the same. Gainful employment o' the
ol' grey matter is takin' an unfair
advantage, apparently. An' that ain't
cricket. Ain't British. Ergo, rational
debate is fairly an' squarely plonked back
where they like to keep it. On the playing
fields of Eton. Know what I mean?

VIV: Not really.

TONE: I shoulda thought it was crystal clear.

Beat.

VIV: My mum once told me that the fact that I didn't believe in God was evidence of my own limited imagination.

TONE: Yeah. There's only one thing I 'ate more than a Christian.

VIV: What's that?

TONE: A glib Christian.

Beat.

VIV: She also told me to respect other people's beliefs.

TONE: Impeccable bloody liberal, your mum. Why? Respect?

VIV: I dunno. 'Cause it takes courage?

TONE: So does jumpin' out of a plane without a parachute. Don't earn you a lot o' respect, though.

VIV: Can't you talk about it without . . .

TONE: Descending to cliché?

VIV: Quite.

TONE: No, I meant you were . . .

VIV: Charming.

TONE: Not at all. Fuckin' rude, I'd say.

VIV: I was using bourgeois understatement.

TONE: I know. I can smell it a mile off. (*Pause.* VIV *takes out dope gear and rolls a joint.*) I've tried, y'know. Prayin'. Seriously . . . When I 'ad a bit of spiritual crisis. I went down on me knees, clenched tight, and I asked God if he had any ideas on the theory of surplus value. An' did e'? Not a sausage. So. That left me with two possible conclusions: One, God doesn't exist. Two, God exists, but 'e's never read Marx. Now, on the basis that two is correct, I can only draw one conclusion: 'Arold Wilson is God. (*Beat.*) Frightenin' innit? (*He finishes his drink and pours a small scotch.*) I went to Sunday School once. Sat there an' cried me eyes out. Never went again. From that moment on, I was a born-again pagan.

Beat.

VIV: Aren't you frightened of dying?

TONE: No. (*Long pause.*) D'you know what I'm frightened of? I'm frightened of Sir Geoffrey Howe. And his new Jerusalem. His Property Owning Democracy. That's what I call death. (*Pause.*) They love it, don't they, our rulers? They love their Christianity. Gives us something to blame. Kids got rickets? Bugger. Ol' God again, up to 'is tricks. Lost your job? Believe in God an' die 'appy. 'Alf the world starves while the other 'alf over-consumes? Funny ol' world innit? Still, blame God. An' don't try 'avin' a go at 'im about all this death an' destruction, 'cause 'e ain't fuckin' there! Well, 'e is, but 'e ain't. Get it? Good, now toddle along an' don't ask no more stupid questions. An' we do! We all toddle along. A conspiracy of ignorance. An' 'cause *we're* all past 'elp anyway, all our bright-eyed missionaries an' would-be martyrs trot off an' take it, like rabies, to another lot of unsuspectin', thick, punters. 'The West suckin' *your* country dry? Not got enough to eat? Never mind. Read this bible. Tells you all about 'ow it's got to 'appen 'cause God made the world an' business believes in God. An' you'll love the miracles, you bein' a bit primitive an' all.' I tell you, when I see all those smug vicars an' smilin' nuns an' serene fuckin' monks I feel sick. They're so proud. Proud they got the answer. Proud we 'respect their courage.' Proud they're immune. (*Beat.*) Honest, sometimes I could murder Cliff Richard. (*Pause.*) I'm an extremist, y'see.

VIV: Oh.

TONE: Yeah. Oh. No compromise. No accommodation. I don't suffer fools gladly. Loony left. I won't drown in the waters of the middle ground. (*Beat.*) My other hobbies include mixing metaphors and getting drunk.

Pause.

VIV: Where's Jane?

TONE: Upstairs, workin'.

VIV: When do her exams start?

TONE: Six, seven weeks, I dunno.

VIV: And what are your feelings on that?

TONE: On what?

VIV: A girlfriend who's training to be a solicitor?

TONE: Up to 'er. There's law an' there's law. (*He takes out a couple of pills, blue, and swallows them.*)

VIV: What's that?

TONE: Speed.

VIV: Wouldn't have thought you needed it.

TONE: I'm a very shy, retiring boy, really. (*Beat.*) Better'n that stuff. Last thing I need's slowin' down.

VIV: Helps me relax.

TONE: So, who wants to relax? 'Specially today.

VIV: What's so special about today?

TONE: Today, with any luck, is the day we tell 'Operation Swamp' to stuff it.

VIV: Operation what?

TONE: Swamp, darlin'. Swamp. Ring any bells? Remember the phrase, 'swamped by an alien culture?' Remember who said that?

VIV: No.

TONE: The copper's friend. Margaret Thatcher. Accordin' to 'er penetratin' analysis, we are in danger of bein' swamped by an alien culture. Viz: nasty darkies in Brixton. Hence: 'Operation Swamp.' Christ. Where you bin?

VIV: Camden.

Pause.

TONE: You, er, notice anythin' outside?

VIV: Like what?

TONE: Like, more coppers 'n a Freemason's ball?

VIV: Oh. The police.

TONE: Yeah. The police.

VIV: I did notice one or two.

TONE: One or two? Thass an army of occupation. An' armies start wars.

VIV: I find it hard to think of a few policemen as an army of occupation.

TONE: You ain't black.

VIV: Neither are you.

TONE: 'S not the point. You own a house. A nice house. Unfortunately, you're gonna be right slap bang in the middle when it all goes up. You'll be lookin' to the police for 'elp.

VIV: That *is* what they're there for.

TONE: Nah. Christ, I thought you went to University. The police force was created to protect the property an' persons o' the middle an' upper classes from the poor people o' the slums. Dixon o' Dock Green didn't just sort of evolve outa the primeval slime. He was made. For a reason. A bloody great patch on the rotten social fabric. (*Beat.*) An' 'e's carryin' on 'is 'istoric mission out there now. Tonight. Liftin' anyone wiv a black face for whatever reason he cares to make up. It's known as positive policing. An' it's a mistake. There's gonna be 'ell to pay. (*Pause.*) Anyway. I feel like a jolly-up. (*He goes to the door and shouts:*) Jane.

JANE (*off*): Coming.

TONE: I'm off.

VIV: I don't think you'll get your war.

TONE: I'll huff an' I'll puff an' I'll . . .

JANE enters.

JANE: What are you doing?

TONE: Goin' over the boozer.

JANE: What for?

TONE: A drink? Make sense?

JANE: I thought we were going to have a meal.

TONE: 'Nother time. I gotta meet Lloyd.

JANE: Bloody Lloyd. Why don't you go *out* with Lloyd? He sees more of you than I do.

TONE: Nah. I've 'ad 'im. 'E's rubbish. (*Beat.*) C'mon, doll. This is important.

JANE: So you keep telling me.

Pause.

TONE: I'll catch you later. (*He kisses her.*)

JANE: I might be out.

He stops and smiles at her, then goes.

VIV: Men. (*Pause.*) Drink?

JANE: Yeah. Why not.

VIV *pours two scotches and hands one to* JANE. *She clinks the glasses.*

VIV: Cheers.

JANE: Cheers.

Pause.

VIV: How's work going?

JANE: Boring. Company law. Who needs it?

VIV: Companies? (*They smile.*) Lovely earrings.

JANE: Oh, I made them.

VIV: They really go with your eyes.

JANE: Thanks. I could make you a pair if you want.

VIV: Have to be a different colour. To go with my eyes. Something small and pinky.

JANE: Your eyes are a lovely colour.

VIV: And what colour, exactly, would you say that was? I've never been able to make my mind up about that.

JANE (*looking into her eyes*): Sort of . . .

VIV: See? Nondescript.

JANE: No. Sort of . . . browny grey.

VIV: Sludge.

JANE: No.

VIV: Mud.

JANE: Browny grey. What's wrong with that?

VIV: It's not a colour, that's what's wrong with it.

Pause.

JANE: Been shopping?

VIV: Yeah. Camden Lock. I went mad. Spent fifty quid.

JANE: No.

VIV: Yeah.

JANE: How can you afford it?

VIV: I can't. But I got some lovely things. Look (*She takes out a jacket.*) I just bought whatever I fancied. Trousers. (*She takes the things out.*) Jumper for work. If I ever get any. Some T-shirts.

JANE: I like the trousers.

VIV: Annie's got a pair almost the same.

JANE: They're nice. I've seen them.

VIV: Nice on Annie. probably make me look like a horse.

JANE: 'Course they won't.

VIV: If I try them on, will you give me an honest opinion? 'Cause I can take them back if I don't like them.

JANE: They'll be fine.

VIV: I may need your help, Jane. (*Pause. VIV puts the trousers on. They won't do up.*) I *do* need your help. (*She takes a deep breath as JANE yanks the zip up.*)

JANE: There.

VIV (*breathing out*): Oh . . . God . . . (*She laughs.*) Is it worth it?

JANE: They'll stretch. (*VIV undoes the button, takes a deep breath and does it up again.*) OK?

VIV: Mmm. What do they look like?

JANE: Fine.

VIV: Be a bit more positive.

JANE: They look great.

VIV: Am I the most beautiful woman you've ever seen?

JANE: You are, without doubt, the most beautiful woman in the world.

VIV: You're saying this of your own free will?

JANE: Would I lie to you?

VIV: End the conversation there, I think. (*She laughs.*) Oh. Look, I bought this. (*She holds up a T-shirt.*) I know it doesn't suit me. D'you want it?

JANE: It's yours. Put it on.

VIV (*holding it up against herself*): Look. (*The T-shirt is very flashy.*) If that's me, I must be someone else.

JANE: Try it on.

VIV: So you can have a good laugh? (*She takes her top off and puts the T-shirt on.*) Oh, repulsive. Here. (*She takes it off and throws it to JANE.*)

JANE: You sure?

VIV: Sure, I'm sure.

JANE *takes off her top. VIV stares. JANE puts the T-shirt on.*

JANE: Well?

VIV, *walks around* JANE *arranging the shirt.*

VIV: It's yours.

JANE: How much was it?

VIV: Only a couple of quid.

JANE: Let me give it to you.

VIV: Don't worry.

JANE: No. I insist. (*She gets the money from her purse and hands it to* VIV.)

VIV: It was supposed to be a present. (*Pause.*) Another drink?

JANE: No, I've got to work.

VIV: One more won't hurt. (*She purrs.*) Cheers.

JANE: Cheers. You'll catch cold.

VIV: Mmm? Oh no. Not only do I look like a horse, but I've got the constitution of an ox.

JANE: You shouldn't be so negative.

VIV *gets up and walks to the door.*

VIV: I'll try to think beautiful thoughts.

VIV *goes out.* JANE *puts the scotch bottle away, thinks, and takes off the T-shirt. She examines the price label.* VIV *comes back in.*

JANE: A couple of quid? Five seventy-five.

VIV: Was it? Oh well.

JANE: Viv . . .

VIV: Sssh. (*She puts her finger to* JANE's *lips and smiles.*) Please? (JANE *puts the T-shirt back on.* VIV *gives her a gentle hug.*) It's nice. Very you. (*She looks around, puzzled, then looks all round the room.*)

JANE: What've you lost?

VIV: Have you hidden it or something?

JANE: What?

VIV: The scotch.

JANE: I put it back in the cupboad.

VIV: Why?

JANE: I dunno.

VIV: I want some more.

JANE: It's only in the cupboard.

VIV: I didn't put it there.

Pause.

JANE: Sorry.

She gets the bottle and holds it out to VIV. VIV *holds out her glass. Pause.* JANE *takes the top off the bottle and pours. They look at each other.* VIV *takes a swig.*

VIV: Have one yourself.

JANE: I . . . might go over the pub.

VIV: Chasing after Tone? Bad move. I'm meeting the others at 'Rumours' in Covent Garden. Why don't you come?

JANE: No thanks.

Pause.

VIV: You should come out with us sometimes.

JANE: I've got too much work. Anyway, I don't like trooping around in a gang.

VIV: A gang. Is that what we are?

JANE: I don't mean . . . Well, you know what I mean.

VIV: I think I do. A gang of what? (*Beat.*) A gang of kids?

JANE: No . . .

VIV: Just a gang. (*Beat.*) I don't want to go to this bloody cocktail bar.

JANE: Don't then.

Pause. Then VIV *laughs.*

VIV: That's right. I don't have to, do I? (*Pause.*) I might as well, though. They're expecting me. The gang. (*Pause.*) 'S a funny thought, isn't it? That this is all mine. The chairs . . . carpet . . . table . . . . saucepans . . . wallpaper . . . Even the dirt in the corners is mine. The ring round the bath is mine. I own it. 'S a funny thought. I mean, what are you supposed to do with it? When you own it? Look. Here it all is . . . And what?

Pause.

JANE: Just live in it.

VIV: Just live in it. What a drag. (*Pause.*) I know. I'll have a party. Haven't had a party for ages. A weekend bash. We'll go on for days. Maybe never stop. Tell your friends. (*Pause.*) What I'd really like is a house with a garden. Chelsea or somewhere. That's what I should aim for.

JANE: Chelsea? Cost the earth.

VIV: My parents . . . My parents look on it as an investment. I'm sort of sitting on their money watching it grow. (*Pause.*) I'd rather watch it grow in Chelsea, frankly. With a garden.

Pause. VIV *stands and starts getting dressed.*

JANE: I'd better get back to work.

VIV: Not going lusting after Tone?

JANE: Not right now, no.

VIV: Good for you. Not worth it, men I mean, look at Rusty . . .

JANE: Rusty?

VIV: I lusted after Rusty. God, did I lust.

JANE: You didn't . . . ?

VIV: Screw him? Did I ever. (*Pause.*) I tend to go off people after I've had sex with them, though. Odd, isn't it?

JANE: Yes. I don't.

VIV: No. You're the deeply faithful type.

Pause.

JANE: I'll probably see you later. If I'm still up.

VIV: Yes.

Pause.

JANE: Thanks for the T-shirt.

VIV: 'S OK.

JANE *goes.* VIV *is now dressed.*

Drinky-poo.

She pours a scotch and drinks. She picks up JANE's *discarded top and gently smells it. Pause. She takes out her new jacket and puts it on. She poses, then flops down in the chair. She looks around.*

Hello room. You're all mine.

Beat.

Fade.

Scene Three

Midnight that night. BAZ *is connecting wires between two reel-to-reel tape recorders.* VIV *and* ANNIE *are making cocktails from a recipe book. They are all very drunk and the women are laughing.*

VIV: You haven't got enough ice.

ANNIE: Bollocks, Viv. There's masses of ice in there.

VIV: Bollocks, Annie. It needs more. (*She goes to the fridge.*)

ANNIE: We're making cocktails, not sinking the Titanic.

VIV *puts more ice in the shaker.*

VIV: There.

ANNIE: You're s'posed to crush it first. Oh Christ. Now we'll have to put more everything in.

VIV: Uh-huh. (*They giggle.* VIV *reads from the book. As she calls them out,* ANNIE *pours them in.*) OK. Dark rum.

ANNIE: Dark rum.

VIV: Light rum.

ANNIE: Light rum.

VIV: Squeeze of lime.

ANNIE: Squeeze of lime.

VIV: Squeeze of lemon.

VIV: Squeeze of lemon.

VIV: Bitters.

ANNIE: Bitters.

VIV: Cointreau.

ANNIE: Cointreau.

VIV: Vodka.

ANNIE: Vodka. Eh?

VIV (*pouring them in as she says them*): Vodka. Gin. Brandy. Martini.

ANNIE: Jesus Christ, Viv. What are you doing?

VIV: This cocktail is my very own invention. The Neutron Bomb. Destroys human flesh, but leaves the house intact.

ANNIE: Don't spill it on the carpet. It'll burn a bloody hole.

VIV: Now . . . We shake (*She shakes it.*) And stand well back and pour. (*She pours four drinks.*) Bit of a funny colour.

ANNIE: You're telling me.

VIV: Ah. Cherries. Where are the cherries? Can't have a cocktail without cherries. Very bad form.

ANNIE: They're here somewhere. (*She turns out the kitchen cupboard. They both laugh.*) Anchovies. Olives (*She holds up a jar.*) Er . . . cockles?

VIV: Cockles? (*Pause.*) Tone!

ANNIE (*holding her nose*): Ugh. (*She puts them back in the cupboard.*)

VIV: Wonder if he's got any winkles?

They laugh. BAZ looks round and shakes his head.

BAZ: Where's me bloody drink?

ANNIE: We're just looking for the cherries, dummy.

BAZ: Well, hurry up. Oh, sod the cherries. (*He goes to take his glass.*)

VIV (*holding them up*): Cherries!

ANNIE: Wait wait wait. Cocktail sticks.

VIV: Cocktail sticks . . .

BAZ: Bugger the cocktail sticks. (*He takes a cherry and drops it in his glass.*)

ANNIE: Ooh, you're so couth.

BAZ: I'm in need of a drink, woman. (*He sips.*) Bloody hell fire. (*They laugh.*) What you put in there?

ANNIE: Oh . . . Rum . . .

VIV: Vodka . . .

ANNIE: Vinegar . . .

VIV: Meths . . .

ANNIE: Harpic . . .

BAZ: Bloody tastes like it an' all. I can't drink that.

VIV: 'Course you can. Look. (*She picks up a glass and downs it in one.*) See?

BAZ: You'll kill yourself.

ANNIE: Don't be such a wimp, Baz. (*She downs a glass. Pause.*) Oh . . . My . . . God. (*VIV laughs.*) He's right. I'm gonna die. (*They both laugh.*)

BAZ: You're both round the twist.

RUSTY *enters.*

RUSTY: Baz, haven't you got it fucking set up yet?

BAZ: No, I fucking haven't.

RUSTY: How long does it take, for Christ's sake?

BAZ: Do it your bloody self.

RUSTY: Darling, you're the one with the magic screwdriver, right? (VIV *and* ANNIE *giggle.*) Oh, for crying out loud.

ANNIE: Have a drink.

RUSTY: If you insist.

VIV: We do.

RUSTY (*takes a sip*): Oh yeah. Very funny. What is it?

ANNIE: It's a bloody cocktail, isn't it?

RUSTY: Yeah? Well maybe it needs a little more eye of newt.

VIV: Of course!

BAZ *goes back to the tape recorders as they start making more cocktails.*

RUSTY: See if you can do a proper one. See if you can manage a 'Between the Sheets.'

ANNIE: Be more than you can. (*They laugh.*)

RUSTY: Pathetic.

ANNIE: Oh, poor old Rusty. Did we hurt his feelings?

VIV: Shall we make it better? (*They both go over to him.*) Where's it hurt, then?

ANNIE: Is it very bad?

VIV: You poor old thing. (*They're both pawing him.*)

VIV: Mmm. Poor old thing.

RUSTY (*ignoring them*): How's it going, Baz?

BAZ: Won't be long.

RUSTY: Good. (*He takes a piece of paper out of his pocket and reads.*)

ANNIE: For God's sake.

VIV: Rotten bastard.

RUSTY: Sorry? D'you say something?

ANNIE: Conceited little rat.

RUSTY: Look, darlings, I'm just going to put some words over a backing track, right? It won't take very long. And when I've finished, you'll have my undivided attention, OK?

ANNIE (*to* VIV): Don't hold your breath.

VIV: I'm gonna make another cocktail.

(*She goes back to the drinks.*)

ANNIE (*to* RUSTY): Why d'you have to do that now?

RUSTY: I promised Phil I'd give it to him tomorrow.

ANNIE: Can't he wait?

RUSTY: No.

ANNIE: It's only a piddling song.

RUSTY: It's not only a piddling song! (ANNIE *blows a raspberry.*) Baz!

BAZ: All right!

RUSTY: Christ!

JANE *enters.*

JANE: Hi. Sounds like you're having fun.

VIV *and* ANNIE *are immediately more subdued.*

VIV: We're doing some cocktails. Have a taste.

JANE: Is it very strong?

ANNIE: Wouldn't be a cocktail if it wasn't, would it?

JANE: S'pose not. Well. (*She sips.*) Crumbs. Not for me.

VIV: Chicken.

JANE: You actually drinking that?

VIV: Drinking it? We're awash with it. (*She finishes off the glass and pours some more.*)

RUSTY: They're being really heroic. Dead impressive.

ANNIE: I'd tell you to drop dead if you didn't give the impression that you already have.

VIV (*serious*): Rusty, we're s'posed to be having a party. It's s'posed to be fun. This is my house, and when I say everybody have fun, then everybody has fun.

RUSTY: Fun. Right. (*He suddenly picks up the glasses and drains them, drinks from the shaker and bottles as:*) Hey! This is great! I'm having a great time! Whoopee! Fun fun fun!! (*Pause. Out of breath:*) How's that? (*Pause. VIV suddenly slaps him on the shoulder.*) Hey, that hurts.

VIV: Good.

She slaps again and again, pushing him

onto the sofa. He starts hitting her back. They struggle. He tickles her. She giggles and suddenly kisses him. He kisses her back.

ANNIE: Someone give Ken Russell a ring, he'd love this.

She grabs RUSTY *and joins in.* BAZ, *headphones on, is still busy with the tapes.* JANE *stands, faintly embarrassed, uncertain what to do. Then she goes over to them.*

JANE: If Tone comes in, can you tell him . . ?

RUSTY *grabs her and pulls her over. She becomes part of the melee, but pulls herself away and stands up.*

Yeah. Great fun.

She goes. Pause. They all burst out laughing.

ANNIE: Got rid of her.

RUSTY: Can't we get her back?

VIV: No.

ANNIE: Uptight bitch.

VIV: I need a drink.

RUSTY: I know what I need.

ANNIE: Tough titty.

RUSTY: Oh, come on.

ANNIE: Gotta do your backing track, haven't you?

RUSTY: I'm putting my voice over the backing track, stupid.

ANNIE: Same difference.

RUSTY: It can wait.

ANNIE (*going over to* VIV): Right. What shall we put in this one?

VIV: Arsenic. We'll all commit ritual suicide on poisoned cocktails.

ANNIE: What a lovely way to go.

VIV: We could get in the car and just drive, knowing we only had ten minutes to live. Leave now, in the dark, never see the sun again. Hit the motorway, never see the end. Ever.

ANNIE: Let's not get morbid, dear.

VIV: It's the booze.

ANNIE: No, it's not. It's you. (*Pause.*) C'mon. We're s'posed to be having fun.

VIV: Yeah. (*She downs a drink in one.*) Come on.

ANNIE *does the same.*

ANNIE: We need a top up.

VIV: How right you are.

RUSTY: Look girls, you're gonna make yourselves ill.

ANNIE: So who gives a flying one?

RUSTY: I do. I'm the one who's gotta sleep with it, right?

ANNIE: No one's forcing you. You're not exactly gonna be dragged screaming into bed.

RUSTY: Oh. I was rather hoping . . .

ANNIE: Ha ha. Look, if you don't like it . . .

RUSTY: I know what I can do.

ANNIE: Yeah. Don't forget.

VIV: She can always sleep in my bed.

ANNIE *puts her arm round* VIV.

ANNIE (*to* RUSTY): I don't need you.

RUSTY: Stop playing games.

VIV: Who's playing games?

RUSTY: You're gonna feel very silly in the morning.

ANNIE: How do you know?

Pause.

VIV: You should be nicer to us. Treat us with a little more respect. We're a little bit fed up with being used, y'know. A little bit miffed that you seem to think we're only here for your benefit. (*Pause.*) You like to break the rules, Rusty. So do we. Don't we?

ANNIE: Yeah.

Pause. They kiss.

VIV: See?

RUSTY (*dry*): Revolutionary. Real fifth form stuff. (*Pause.*) Honestly, girls, I'm not impressed.

BAZ (*taking off the headphones and turning round*): All set to go.

Pause.

RUSTY: About time.

BAZ: All set to go? Thanks, Baz. That's all right, Rusty. Anything for a pal. (*Pause.*) Just don't ask again.

RUSTY: What is this? Open season? I mean, what did I do?

ANNIE: You breathed.

Pause.

RUSTY: OK. Whatever it is I've done to offend everyone . . . I'm sorry. Right? Now, please, just get off my back.

Pause.

ANNIE: Well . . . He did say sorry.

VIV: Only just.

ANNIE: Well, it *was* his first time.

VIV: Frighten you, did we?

Pause.

BAZ: Look, I'll play this . . . (*He switches on the tape recorder. Music comes out: electro-synthesizer pop style.*) . . . OK? Now, you wear the headphones and you sing into this mike, which then records your voice over the voice and backing track that's already there. Got it?

RUSTY: What d'you think I am? An idiot?

ANNIE: Don't answer that.

BAZ: Have you got it?

RUSTY: 'Course I've got it.

BAZ: Right. I'll just wind back to the beginning, then you're ready.

RUSTY: OK.

VIV: What's the song called?

RUSTY (*self-conscious*): 'The Shock of the New.'

VIV: Catchy.

RUSTY: Look, don't put me off while I'm doing it, will you?

ANNIE: Wouldn't dream of it.

VIV: D'you want us to stand out of the way?

RUSTY: Yeah, that's cool.

VIV: Must do what the man says, Annie.

They stand by the window, every now and then breaking into laughter.

RUSTY: And don't make any noise. It'll come out on the tape.

ANNIE: Ssssh

RUSTY puts the headphones on. The girls giggle.

RUSTY: I heard that.

They stand, trying not to laugh. BAZ switches on the tape. RUSTY clicks his fingers in time with the music. He looks unsure where to begin. He starts.

There's a – fuck it. (*They laugh.*) Sorry, Baz. I wasn't sure where it started. Back to the beginning?

BAZ: You know where to come in?

RUSTY: Yeah. I got it now. (BAZ *starts the tape again.* RUSTY *clicks his fingers and starts to sing.*) 'There's a –'

The door flies open and TONE rushes in. He's wearing gloves and a bandana round his neck.

For fuck's sake!

BAZ, ANNIE *and* VIV *are in hysterics.*

TONE: What 'appened to the milk bottles?

RUSTY: Milk bottles?!

TONE: Yeah. There was a load 'ere.

RUSTY: How should we know where they are?!

TONE *looks and finds them in a plastic bag.*

VIV: What d'you want the milk bottles for?

TONE: Cocktails.

He goes.

RUSTY: Stupid prick. OK, Baz. Try again.

VIV *and* ANNIE *peer through the blinds.* RUSTY *puts the headphones on.* VIV *gets* ANNIE *and herself a drink. The tape starts.* RUSTY *clicks his fingers and sings:*

There's a finger on my pulse / And the pulse is getting weak / Hold your head back / Look around / People dying / What's that sound / It's heading for you / It's the shock of the new / Can you feel it too / It's the shock of the new. Lights are going out / Walls falling down / You ask yourself / What did I do / Your eyes are shut / They're stuck like glue / To the shock of the new / And it's heading for

you / Can you feel it too / It's the shock of the new.

During the last verse and chorus we hear police sirens outside. ANNIE, VIV *and* BAZ *stare out.* RUSTY *is oblivious.*

You can't resist / So don't fight back / You can't resist / So don't fight back / That's their game / They'll suck you in / They'll chain you in / Eternal sin

JANE *enters.* RUSTY *continues*:

But it's heading for you / It's the shock of the new / Can you feel it too / It's the shock of the new.

RUSTY *keeps clicking his fingers till the song ends, then he hears the sirens. He pulls off the headphones. They turn and look at him, frightened.*

JANE: It's a riot.

Pause.

RUSTY: THEY RUINED MY SONG!

Blackout.

Scene Four

4 a.m. next morning. The room is dark, dawn just coming in through the window. VIV *is sitting in the chair. The front door slams off stage. The door opens.* TONE *enters. He goes to the fridge, takes out a can of beer and opens it. He turns on the light. There is a small trickle of blood on his forehead. He sees* VIV. *Pause.*

TONE: Still up?

Pause. She holds up a large kitchen knife.

Doin' yer nails? (*Pause.*) Whassat in aid of, then? (*Pause.*) Ah. this must be what Jane calls your broody silence. (*Pause.*)

VIV: Does she talk about me a lot?

TONE: Not 'specially.

VIV: What does she say about me?

TONE: Nothin'.

Pause.

VIV: I feel threatened.

TONE: I 'ad gathered that. (*Pause.*) 'S no need. No one's gonna break in 'ere.

VIV: How do I know?

TONE: 'S all dyin' down now. Everyone's knackered. (*Pause.*) You bin out?

VIV: No.

TONE: Should 'ave. Quite an experience.

VIV: 'D you enjoy yourself?

TONE: A wonderful time was had by all.

VIV: You should be shot. (*Pause.*) You've cut your head.

TONE: Yeah. Pretty rotten trick, as it 'appens. There we are, lobbin' rocks at the ol' bill, an' they start lobbin' 'em back. Crack. I catch one on the bonce.

VIV: Good. (TONE *smiles.*) What's funny?

Pause.

TONE: Want some beer?

VIV: No. (*Pause.*) I could arrest you. Citizen's arrest. Hand you over.

TONE: What for?

VIV: You're dangerous. Might be about to rob the house. I could stab you. Self defence. You could be a rapist. Who knows? (*Pause.*) Pour me a scotch.

TONE: Nope. (*Pause.*) If I pour you a scotch, will you put the knife away?

VIV: Nope! (*Pause.*) You know my parents live in California?

TONE: Yeah?

VIV: They have a gun. Two. One each.

TONE: 'S only fair.

VIV: Yes. (*Pause.*) Please will you pour me a scotch?

TONE: I think you've already 'ad a few.

VIV: I've been drinking all day. I've drunk myself sober. Please.

He gets up and pours a scotch. As he hands it to her, she slowly cuts the back of his hand with the knife. He holds the glass out to her. Pause. She takes it.

Thank you.

He takes the scarf from his neck and wraps it round his hand.

TONE: You can put it away now. (VIV *smiles.*)

VIV: Are you frightened?

TONE: Of you?

VIV: Yes.

TONE: Leave it out.

VIV: What if I stabbed you?

TONE: I'd put it down to experience.

VIV: You'd bleed.

TONE: That too.

VIV: You deserve to bleed.

TONE: I ain't doin' too badly so far. (*Pause.*) Not gettin' on very well, are we?

VIV: No. I think it's because we despise each other.

TONE: I'll go along wi' that.

Pause.

VIV: It's a bit of a nerve, isn't it? Coming into my house, spreading your trail of disgust around. Like a slug. Everywhere you look, a little silver trail. I'd say it's a bit of a nerve.

TONE: Would you?

VIV: Yes. (*Pause.*) You make me think of creepy crawlies. Things that make your skin creep. Slugs. Leeches. Spiders. Things that live in your house whether you want them there or not. Things you leave little traps for. Chemicals. If I pour salt on you, will you shrivel up?

TONE: Maybe.

VIV: That'd be nice. To watch your skin bubble and melt. Slowly pouring on more until you were dead. It takes a long time. Oh, the pain.

TONE: Like that, would you?

VIV: Very much.

Pause.

TONE: Pretty little mind you got there.

VIV: I like it. (*Pause.*) I wouldn't think things like that if you weren't here. It's really your own fault. I mean, I've not been inhospitable. I've let Jane have you here. And all you've done is shit on us.

TONE: What I do outside these four walls, what I am, is none o' your business. None at all.

VIV: But, you're not outside these four walls, are you? I mean . . Here you are. And what you are is my business. You squat there like you own the place. Looking down your nose at us. Sneering. Superior.

TONE: An' we can't 'ave two of us lookin' like we own the place, can we?

VIV: I do own it.

TONE: Here endeth the lesson.

VIV: Talk to me! Don't sit there making statements, sneering.

TONE: I don't wanna talk to you. What's the point? All I get is abuse.

VIV: Abuse is all you know. A steady trickle, hidden away, very subtle. But all the time, you're trying to dig away, scratching holes in my life.

TONE: You can't scratch holes in a string vest.

VIV: You can tell Jane I don't want you here any more.

TONE: Tell 'er yourself. It's 'er decision.

VIV: It's my decision.

TONE: Look, just because mummy an' daddy own the bricks an' mortar, don't mean you got any say in 'ow Jane runs 'er life.

VIV: We've all got to live here.

TONE: Oh, finally noticed, 'ave yer? I was beginnin' to think this was your own private party. No gatecrashers allowed. That's 'ow you think o' me, innit? Wasn't invited, didn't bring a bottle, doesn't join in. Well, honestly, darlin', I don't wanna join in wi' the crummy little scene you got 'ere. I'm 'ere 'cause Jane asked me to come. As is 'er right. Now, if you don't like it, I suggest you learn to live wiv it, or stick it. (*Pause.*) Can't understand it, can yer? Everyone else treats you like yer the belle o' the ball. They respect you, don't they? That's what you'd like to think. Dead popular, you are. An' I can tell 'ow much you want that. Not surprisin', really. I mean, if I was like you, I'd wanna be loved. I'd pretend, like you. I s'pose I'd 'ate me as well, 'cause . . . see . . . I respect people, not the things they own. An' you 'ave to earn respect, which is prob'ly where you fall down. I mean, when 'ave you ever 'ad to earn anything? (*Pause.*) Least I can stop pretendin', now. I don't 'ave to be polite any more, pretend I can actually stand bein' in the same fuckin' room as you. (*Pause.*) Message ends.

Pause.

VIV: You don't know the first thing about me.

TONE: Got 'idden depths, 'ave you?

Pause.

VIV: Get out.

TONE: In me own good time.

VIV: Get out. Or I'll call the police.

TONE: I wouldn't do that. I reckon they'd be quite interested in some o' the substances in common use round 'ere.

Pause.

VIV: I don't think I like people very much.

TONE: Awkward, ain't they? Minds o' their own. Bit of a bugger, eh?

VIV: You've got no right to say any of this.

TONE: Talk to me, you said. So, I'm talkin'. Sorry you don't like what you 'ear.

VIV: You really think I don't know? What I am? You really think I don't hate myself?

TONE: Shows good judgement.

VIV: Don't. Please.

TONE: Don't expect me to go all soft 'cause you finally own up to the truth. You'll be your ol' self again tomorrow. 'Ave to be. Otherwise, 'ow could you go on? (*Pause.* VIV *looks at him, then puts the knife to her wrist.*) Let's not get silly. (*Pause.*) You ever seen a corpse? (*She shakes her head.*) No. Me, neither. Don't reckon I missed much.

He stands and calmly takes the knife from her. She takes his hand and holds it gently.

VIV: Sorry I cut you. (*He pulls his hand away.*)

TONE: Piss off. (*He looks through the blind.*)

Pause.

VIV: You'd probably have to leave anyway. I'm thinking about moving to Chelsea. A smaller place. I'm thinking quite seriously about it.

TONE: Good for you.

VIV: Yeah. This place is a bit of a handful, y'know . . .

TONE: Actually, let you into a little secret – Chelsea's next on the list. 'Ad it planned for ages, we 'ave. So maybe it's not such a good idea, Chelsea. (*Pause.*) Ever thought of emigratin'?

VIV: Leave me alone!

TONE: Just bein' practical.

VIV: I'll go wherever I have to to get away from all this.

TONE: All this? What about all that? (*He points to the window.*) Look. Look outside. There's people there. People 'oo actually live 'ere. Not playn'. Not practisin' for the suburbs. Livin'. (*Pause.*) You've 'ad a nice break. P'raps now you oughta go back where you feel safe.

VIV: This is my country. I'll live where I like.

TONE: I s'pose it's mummy an' daddy's country too, is it? Livin' in America, earnin' a packet, buyin' up 'ouses for you to 'ide yerself in.

VIV: This is also a free country. People can do what they like with their money.

TONE: If they 'appen to 'ave any.

Pause.

VIV: What am I supposed to say? Sorry? Or what? (*Pause.*) I'm sorry I don't do anything? I don't contribute? Sorry my way's been smooth for me since the start? That I'm perfect? I've turned out just the way I'm supposed to. I don't think much. I'm ideal. (*Pause.*) What have I got? A degree? I can understand French movies and read the quality papers? Sorry I want to end up at the BBC with all my friends? Custom bred, with our minds perfectly trained to jump fences and stay the course? Because what else is there? Sorry I'm nothing? Our precious freedom's made me a zombie? (*Beat.*) Freedom to rot, that's all this country's given me. (*Pause.*) Is that what you want me to say?

TONE: You fuckin' said it.

VIV: But did I mean it?

BAZ *enters in his dressing-gown and Sony Walkman. He sees them and takes the headphones off.*

BAZ: Still up then? Christ. I need an Alka-Seltzer. Where are they?

VIV: On the shelf. (BAZ *gets the Alka-Seltzer.*) What are you doing up?

BAZ: Phone call. San Francisco. Frisbee is big business. (*He notices* TONE *holding the knife.*) Uh . . . Don't tell me . . . Jack the Ripper.

TONE: Spot on.

Pause. BAZ *looks at his watch.*

BAZ: I've gotta be at Crystal Palace in three hours' time.

TONE: What for?

BAZ: First day of the UK Frisbee Championship. I'm in charge. I can think of better ways of spending a Monday morning.

TONE: So can I.

BAZ: Like, in bed.

TONE: So chuck it.

BAZ: It happens to be my job. If I don't turn up, I get the sack. And if I get the sack, I lose the car and my expenses-paid holiday in sunny California in August.

TONE: Middle-management of the world unite. You've nothin' to lose but your perks.

BAZ: I like that. I think I'll write that up in the office. (VIV *gets up.*) You going to bed?

VIV: No.

She goes off.

BAZ: Is this an argument or something?

TONE: Compulsory re-education.

BAZ: Eh?

TONE: Nothin'.

Pause.

BAZ: Doesn't do to argue with Viv.

TONE: D'you spend your 'ole life duckin' for cover?

BAZ: More or less.

TONE: You oughta toughen up, mate.

BAZ: What for? I'm very comfortable. I can't think of a single reason why I should upset the routine.

TONE: Because it's a routine, maybe?

BAZ: No. I find routine very . . .

TONE: Comfortable.

BAZ: Yeah. (*Pause.*) It's not really your place to say anything, y'know. It's not as if you live here. (*Pause.*) Well is it?

Pause.

TONE: This belonging thing, it's a bloody obsession. You block the 'ole world off wiv it. Middle class barricade, thass all this 'ouse is.

BAZ: I don't think it's unreasonable to ask people to be considerate when they're in your house.

TONE: 'Course you don't. You're a fuckin' lapdog.

BAZ: Well. That's how you see it.

TONE: 'S 'ow you see it an' all.

BAZ (*sarcastic*): We can't all be as aware as you, Tone.

Pause.

TONE: No, you can't, can you?

Pause. He gets up. VIV *comes back in. He hands her the knife.*

'Ere. Do us all a favour. Use it.

He goes. She looks at BAZ *then at the knife and makes a gesture of puzzlement. Then she calmly puts the knife in a drawer and sits down.*

BAZ: Off then, is he?

VIV: Yeah, for good.

BAZ: Oh.

VIV: What else could I do? He suddenly went into this great rant. Really chewed my head off. And he frightens me. He as good as said we'd be attacked if I threw him out.

BAZ: Attacked?

VIV: The riots.

BAZ: Bloody hell.

VIV: But I won't be threatened. Not in my own house.

BAZ: What brought it all on?

VIV: Search me. One minute I'm sitting here having a quiet drink, the next . . .

BAZ: Where'd the knife come from?

VIV: Must have taken it out with him. The man's a lunatic. Luckily, I calmed him down a bit. Otherwise, God knows what might have happened.

BAZ: You should have called me.

VIV: I nearly did. I knew you were there if I needed you.

BAZ: I'm always here.

VIV: Thanks, Baz. (*Pause.*) I've never met anyone that resentful, that jealous of other people.

BAZ: Are you OK?

VIV: Yeah, just about.

BAZ: Sure?

RUSTY: Yeah. Don't worry about me. (*Pause.*) Look, Baz . . . What shall I do about Jane?

BAZ: How d'you mean?

VIV: Well . . . Some of the things he said . . . It was like he was speaking for both of them.

BAZ: What things?

VIV: They despise us, we've got a crummy little scene, we're just a gang of kids.

BAZ: Well, what d'you want to do about her?

VIV: I don't know. It'll just be very heavy living with her here, don't you think?

BAZ: She's pretty easy going.

VIV: But I couldn't stand it. Looking at her, knowing what she's thinking, knowing she despises us . . .

BAZ: I'm sure she doesn't.

VIV: You didn't hear the things he said.

BAZ: No.

Pause.

VIV: If I ask her to move out, will you support me?

Pause.

BAZ: Do what you want. It's your house.

VIV: Yeah. It is, isn't it? (*Pause.*) It's time I was firmer, don't you think?

BAZ: Up to you, Viv.

VIV: Yes, definitely. I won't be abused in my own house. (*Pause.*) So long as you think I'm doing the right thing.

The phone rings. BAZ *picks it up.*

BAZ: Baz here. Hi, Max. (VIV *starts tidying up.*) Eh? (*Pause.*) What d'you mean, they're not coming? (*Pause.*) Oh, Jesus. (*Pause.*) There's more important things in the world than money. Didn't you tell them that? (*Pause.*) Well that's something, I s'pose. When do they get here? (*Pause.*) Tuesday. Is this definite now? (*Pause.*) Well no, but I'll see what I can salvage. (*Pause.*) Yeah. OK. Bye. (*He puts the phone down.*) Bastards.

VIV: What's the matter?

BAZ: The star attractions won't be turning up till the day after tomorrow. They've been offered more money to do an exhibition in Chicago?

VIV: Are they important?

BAZ: They're only the world pairs champions. Nothing special. (*Pause.*) They'll all be doing it now. I'm slinging this job. (*Pause.*) Anyway, we'll have to sort all this out tomorrow. (*Beat.*) Fuck it.

He goes to the door.

VIV: Baz! You're a friend.

BAZ: Eh? (*Beat.*) Oh. Don't be soft.

He goes. She smiles. She picks up TONE's *beer can, holds it gingerly at arm's length and takes it to the waste bin.*

VIV: Goodbye. (*She drops the can in the bin.*)

Beat.

End of Act One

ACT TWO

Scene One

One week later. Midday. BAZ is alone in the room, on the phone.

BAZ: Listen, if it was up to me . . . (*Pause.*) I just run the bloody company. It's not my decision. (*Pause.*) So what do I tell the organisers tomorrow? (*Pause.*) Ha ha. (*Pause.*) For Christ's sake, Ron, see sense.

Pause. The door opens and ANNIE, carrying a wrapped picture, comes in. BAZ waves to her. She nods and puts the picture down, then goes to the kitchen area. He puts his hand over the mouthpiece.

There's coffee on the stove. (*Back into the phone:*) Look, let me speak to Joey, will you? (*Pause.*) Why not? (*Pause.*) Meditating? (*Pause.*) Levitating? (*Pause.*) You mean to tell me that I can't speak to one of my employees because at this moment in time he's in the bedroom floating two feet above the ground? (*Pause.*) OK. I'll get on to Lawrence and see what I can do. (*Pause.*) Well maybe he'll listen to me. (*Pause.*) Yeah. I'll ring you straight back. OK. See you. (*He puts the phone down.*) Fucking hippies! Frisbee-playing bolshie Yank pricks!

Beat.

ANNIE: Trouble?

BAZ: They're on strike. The stupid bastards are refusing to do the exhibition tomorrow. Honestly, they're s'posed to be Buddhists. Buddhists don't go on strike.

ANNIE: What do they want? Meditation allowance?

BAZ: They reckon they're being ripped off. They reckon we pay 'em a pittance for doing the shows, then we make a killing flogging frisbees afterwards.

ANNIE: And do you?

BAZ: 'Course we do. That's not the point. The point is, they're lucky we pay 'em at all. They get expenses. We feed them. Just for chucking lumps of plastic round a bloody field. Honest, I don't know why

I'm in this game. I'd have joined British Leyland if I'd wanted this hassle. (*Beat.*) Let's see what I can screw out of Lawrence. (*He dials.*) Make yourself at home. (*She sits.*) Bill? Baz. Look, we've got another problem. Ron and the others won't do tomorrow's show unless we promise them more money. (*Pause.*) Yeah. (*Pause.*) Fifty each. (*Pause.*) That's what I said. (*Pause.*) How can I do that? (*Pause.*) And will you? (*Pause.*) It's a bit underhand. (*Pause.*) Yeah, I know. That's business. (*Pause.*) Yeah. I think you're right. Hey, and can we cover next week's show? (*Pause.*) Fine. I'll tell him. OK. Call you back if there's any problem. See you. (*He puts the phone down.*)

ANNIE: Well?

BAZ: We promise to pay them.

ANNIE: But . . .

BAZ: We promise. They do the show, we sack Ron, and everything's back to normal. Simple.

ANNIE: Won't that leave you without any players?

BAZ: No. Cool Hand Ron's the shop steward. The others are out of their heads most of the time. They won't care.

ANNIE: Not very nice, your business.

BAZ: Not my fault. I just do like the man says, and collect the cheque each month. Beats working for a living.

ANNIE: Aren't you going to let Cool Hand Ron know?

BAZ: Later. Let him sweat for a bit. Serve him right. (*Pause.*) What are you doing here, anyway?

ANNIE: Thanks. It's nice to feel welcome.

BAZ: I wasn't expecting you.

ANNIE: I bought this picture round for Viv. I thought she'd be here.

BAZ: No . . . she's gone out.

Pause.

ANNIE: Don't be coy. You mean *they've* gone out.

BAZ: Do I?

ANNIE: I assume you do. Unless Rusty's hiding in the cupboard. Which wouldn't surprise me.

BAZ: Yeah. They've gone out.

ANNIE: Oh. Where?

BAZ: Dunno. Raif's?

ANNIE: No. I've just come from there.

BAZ: I see.

ANNIE: Get it where you can, darling, that's my motto. (*Pause.*) I don't mind, y'know. There's no need to look so worried.

BAZ: It's like musical bloody chairs with you lot.

ANNIE: More like postman's knock.

BAZ: How come I never get a go.

ANNIE: You're too nice.

BAZ: I'm a seething animal under this nice exterior.

ANNIE: Probably. That's the trouble. Let's stick with the nice exterior, shall we? Don't spoil a good thing. (*Pause.*) What a schmuck.

BAZ: Rusty?

ANNIE: You guessed.

BAZ: I can see you don't mind.

ANNIE: I don't. It's just he swore blind he wasn't having a thing with Viv. According to Rusty, she's the most boring thing on two legs. Then I get chucked out of the flat, he hasn't got a regular place to doss, and hey, presto, it's true love. God, I don't know how he has the nerve. And Viv. How could she fall for it? (*Pause.*) Anyway, I don't give a damn. Honest. It was hell while it lasted. I wish her well. And I hope he breaks his bloody neck.

BAZ: What about me? I've got him here permanent now. And when Rusty moves in, Rusty moves in.

ANNIE: I know. (*Pause.*) Jane still here, is she?

BAZ: Yeah. Why?

ANNIE: No reason.

Pause.

BAZ: What's everyone got against her?

ANNIE: Who said we've got anything against her?

BAZ: Oh, come on . . .

ANNIE: She's a boring little hausfrau.

BAZ: You *don't* like her, do you?

ANNIE: Whatever gave you that idea?

The phone rings. BAZ picks it up.

BAZ: Hello. (*Pause.*) Ronnie, hi, I was just about to ring you. (*Pause.*) Yeah, I spoke to him. He says OK. (*Pause.*) Yeah. (*Pause.*) What d'you think he's gonna do? Go back on his word? (*Pause.*) Yeah, fifty each. (*Pause.*) Don't thank me. I'm just doing my job. (*Pause.*) Well, I'm glad you're glad. Fine. I'll see you tomorrow. See if you can be there on time, huh? (*Pause.*) And wish Joey a happy landing for me. (*Pause.*) Right. Bye (*Pause.*) You are screwed, you lousy, long-haired little git.

ANNIE: Baz, you are *not* very nice.

BAZ: I told you.

ANNIE: I could almost find you attractive.

BAZ: Now you're talking.

ANNIE: Almost, I said. (*Pause.*) You don't know when they're coming back, by any chance?

BAZ: Couldn't tell you.

ANNIE: Shit. I want the money for the picture.

BAZ: How much?

ANNIE: Normally, I'd charge about fifty. But seeing as it's Viv, I'm letting her have it for seventy-five.

BAZ: For one picture?

ANNIE: Took me a long time. Seventy-five's actually very reasonable.

BAZ: Let's have a look, then.

ANNIE: OK.

She takes it out. It is a glamorous print combining a black and white picture of Hitler's face with heroic swastika flags and the slogan 'Nur Hitler'. She holds it up.

Tell me what you think? (*Beat.*) Well?

BAZ: Really . . . striking.

ANNIE: See, it's two pictures in one, really. The face is taken from a photo and the rest's from a wartime poster I found.

BAZ: Why Hitler?

ANNIE: Forties, dummy. Next big thing. Anyway, I'm fed up with Blondie and Iggy Pop.

BAZ: Where d'you want to put it? (*They look round the room.*) There's a nail there.

ANNIE: OK, let's try it. (*He hangs it. They stare at it.*) What d'you think?

BAZ: Great.

ANNIE: Worth seventy-five pounds of anyone's money, I'd say.

BAZ: 'Specially Viv's. (*Pause.*) You doing anything special today?

ANNIE: No.

Pause.

BAZ: Fancy going out?

ANNIE: No.

Pause.

BAZ: Purely social.

ANNIE: Of course.

BAZ: No, honest.

ANNIE: Look, Baz . . .

BAZ: Don't say it.

Pause.

ANNIE: We wouldn't look right together. You're not my type.

BAZ: Thanks.

ANNIE: No, really, Baz. You have to think about these things. I don't wear clothes that clash, do I? Everything blends. It has to, otherwise you look silly.

BAZ: You talk like people are watching you all the time.

ANNIE: Well, Christ, they are.

Pause.

BAZ: Don't you like me?

ANNIE: I like you a lot.

BAZ: I'm only asking you to come out with me on a Sunday afternoon. For a drive or something.

ANNIE: You're asking me to go to bed with you, and you know it.

Pause.

BAZ: We're not all like Rusty, you know.

ANNIE: Oh, yes you are.

Pause.

BAZ: Forget I asked.

ANNIE: OK.

A door slams offstage.

BAZ: That's probably them. Or noisy burglars.

ANNIE: Yes.

The door opens, VIV *and* RUSTY *come in. No trace of embarrassment.*

VIV: Annie! (*They hug.*) What are you doing here? (ANNIE *points at the picture.*) Oh, great. Wow. Hey, it looks terrific.

ANNIE: Glad you like it.

VIV: Really forties. Rusty reckons the forties are gonna be the next big thing.

ANNIE: Well he should know.

RUSTY *is pouring two scotch and Americans.*

RUSTY: Drink? Or have you got to rush?

ANNIE: No thanks. And I haven't got to rush.

RUSTY: Oh, good. (*He hands* VIV *her drink.*)

BAZ: I'll get my own. (*He does.*)

ANNIE: Hate to say this, Viv, but . . .

VIV: Oh right. (*Getting out her cheque book.*) What did we say? Eighty, was it?

ANNIE: Er . . . yeah.

VIV: Right.

She writes out the cheque and gives it to ANNIE. RUSTY *turns on the video and sorts through some film cassettes.*

RUSTY: Anybody fancy Casablanca?

VIV: Not just now. (*He carries on.*) When are you off to Italy?

ANNIE: Day after tomorrow.

VIV: Lucky thing.

ANNIE: I know. Hey, Nigel says you've got some job or other.

VIV: Sort of. It's just temping. Switchboard on the phone-ins at LBC.

ANNIE: It's something.

VIV: Just. (*The TV comes up very loud.*) Rusty. (*She turns the sound off.*) You can watch it later.

RUSTY: I only wanna look at the clothes. The words are boring.

ANNIE: You know Dennis? He says if this Italian thing goes off all right, he should be able to keep me in work for a while. Said there's even a chance of a job for Cosmo.

VIV: Fantastic.

ANNIE: I know. 'Course, it all depends . . .

VIV: Yeah. (*Pause.*) Why didn't you come round in the week?

ANNIE: I had some things to do. Packing, phone calls, interviews, you know . . .

VIV: We're going to see some band tonight. Coming?

ANNIE: I don't know . . .

VIV: Go on.

ANNIE: Actually, I said I'd go out with Baz. Didn't I, Baz.

BAZ: Eh?

VIV: Where you going?

ANNIE: Oh, that new place . . . The one with the piranha.

VIV: The what?

ANNIE: They've got this glass dance floor; it's bullet proof or something. And underneath, in the water, there's a piranha fish.

VIV: A live one?

ANNIE: Well a dead one wouldn't be much fun, would it?

VIV: I s'pose not.

ANNIE: And, anyway, while you're dancing . . . Under your feet . . . There's this piranha.

Slight pause.

RUSTY: Riots.

VIV: What?

RUSTY: It's called Riots. It's a dump.

ANNIE: We just thought we'd give it a go.

RUSTY: It's all fat Arabs. And the piranha's a goldfish with dentures.

ANNIE: No-one's asking you to come.

RUSTY: Big deal.

Pause.

BAZ: I can't go anyway. I'm having an early night tonight. Sorry.

Pause.

VIV: Come with us.

ANNIE: Don't want to go where I'm not wanted.

VIV: Don't be silly.

Pause.

ANNIE: I'll have to see how I feel.

Pause.

VIV: We've just been and looked at the most fabulous place in Chelsea. Two bedrooms, garden, patio. Great. I've just got to convince the folks they want it.

ANNIE: I don't see what's wrong with this place.

VIV: If things carry on the way they are, this house'll be worth about two pounds fifty in a year's time. I've had the aerial on the car broken twice. It's just so heavy. The riots and everything. I don't feel safe.

RUSTY: What's for lunch?

VIV: Chicken.

RUSTY: When's it gonna be ready?

VIV: I haven't put it in the oven yet.

RUSTY: I'm starving.

VIV: Have a sandwich.

RUSTY: I don't want a sandwich, I want lunch.

VIV: It'll be at least an hour. Why don't you go over the pub?

RUSTY: Yeah, why don't I? (*Pause. She gives him a fiver. He gives her a peck on the cheek.*)

VIV: And I want some change.

RUSTY: Baz? Fancy a drink?

BAZ: You buying? Bloody hell . . .

VIV: About an hour.

RUSTY: Yeah.

RUSTY *and* BAZ *go.*

ANNIE: Well. Who's under whose thumb?

VIV: Nobody.

ANNIE: Come on. It's fatal giving Rusty money. You only give it if you don't expect it back.

VIV: I don't expect it back.

ANNIE: Christ. True love.

VIV: Not at all.

Pause.

ANNIE: I really don't mind, you know. I don't see why we should let a little thing like Rusty come between us. (*They both smile.*)

VIV: Good.

ANNIE: Watch him, though.

VIV: I am.

Pause.

ANNIE: When he first moved in with me, it was twice a night, regular. Then once a night, then once a week, then only months with a 'z' in.

VIV: We're on three times a night at the moment.

ANNIE: Off to a flying start.

VIV: Novelty value, I expect.

ANNIE: Yeah. What'll you do when he slows down?

VIV: Kick him out.

ANNIE: Just don't kick him in my direction.

VIV: No fear.

Pause.

ANNIE: Are you happy?

Pause.

VIV: No. (*Pause.*) Happier. (*Pause.*) It's just not how I want it yet.

ANNIE: Did Che Guevara ever come back?

VIV: I've been keeping out of the way. But, I'm sure he's been here. And she's been really hostile.

ANNIE: Have you spoken to her about it?

VIV: Why should I?

ANNIE: I dunno. Clear the air?

VIV: It's my house. It's my decision. If she doesn't like it she can move out.

ANNIE: Is she in?

VIV: She's probably upstairs, revising. (*Pause.*) God, I hated it when he was here. The perfect bloody couple. Like 'mummy and daddy'.

ANNIE: I did warn you.

VIV: Yeah. (*Pause.*) I mean, what right does she think she has?

ANNIE: Forget it.

VIV: Am I going on?

ANNIE: A bit.

VIV: Sorry. (*The phone rings.* VIV *picks it up.*) Hello. (*Pause.*) I could. Hang on. (*She goes to the door and shouts:*) Jane? Phone.

JANE (*off*): I'll take it up here.

VIV *picks up the phone, listens, then hangs up.*

VIV: Talk of the devil.

ANNIE: Is it him?

VIV: Yeah. Rude sod. I'm not his errand girl. If he thinks he's coming round here . . . (*Pause.*) I better put the chicken in. Are you staying?

ANNIE: I can do.

VIV *takes out a chicken from the fridge, puts it in a baking tin and into the oven.*

VIV: I tried being friends with her. She just doesn't want to know. I don't think she's capable of being friends. She doesn't give anything.

ANNIE: Viv, for God's sake.

VIV: I'll throw a party when you get back From Italy.

ANNIE: Celebrate my suntan.

VIV: Yeah.

JANE *enters with an empty coffee cup and goes to the kitchen.*

JANE: Viv . . . (*She notices* ANNIE.) Hi. Viv, Tone says he's rung a couple of times and you've said I was out.

VIV: Yeah?

JANE: Could you *check* that I'm not in when he rings?

VIV: I do.

JANE: But . . .

VIV: If I say you're out, you're out. I wouldn't say it otherwise, would I?

JANE: I don't know.

VIV: Don't be ridiculous.

JANE: I'm not being ridiculous. I'd just like you to check whether I'm in or not. (VIV *ignores her.*) Viv?

ANNIE: No need to go on.

Pause. JANE *goes round to* VIV, *and notices the picture on the wall.*

Is that supposed to be a joke?

ANNIE: I don't see anybody laughing.

JANE: What's it doing there?

ANNIE: Hanging.

JANE: I can see that. Is it one of yours?

ANNIE: I created it, if that's what you mean.

JANE: Well what's it doing on the fucking wall?

VIV: I PUT IT THERE! I BOUGHT IT! IT'S MY PICTURE, HANGING ON MY WALL! OK?!

Pause.

JANE: Is it deliberate? Because if it is, it worked. (*Pause.*) Please, you can't leave it there. (*Pause.*) Please. (*They ignore her.*) Don't you understand? What it means? (*Beat.*) Look, why don't you just call me Yid. (*Beat.*) I'll wear a yellow star. (*Pause.*) Annie. Doesn't that face mean anything to you? (*Beat.*)

ANNIE: Yeah. About eighty quid.

Pause.

JANE: Is that what you do with everything? Glamorise it. Turn it into another fashion? Millions of deaths? A glamour print? What next? The Auschwitz coffee table book? (*Pause.*) Don't you know what the Nazis did?

ANNIE: Of course I do.

JANE: What?

ANNIE: They killed Jews, I s'pose.

Pause.

JANE: And is that it?

ANNIE: What d'you want me to do? Cry about it?

Pause.

JANE: I feel sorry for you.

ANNIE: Don't bother.

Pause.

JANE: Understand, please. Jewish jokes, swastikas on walls, National Front marches. We've learned to live with all that. But this . . . I don't have to live with this. Not here. (*Pause.*) I'm just asking for a little humanity. (*Long pause.*) Imbeciles. It's hopeless.

JANE goes. VIV pours herself a drink.

ANNIE: I wouldn't mind one of those.

VIV: Why don't you go over the pub?

ANNIE: Why?

VIV: I've got some talking to do. (*Pause.*) How dare she? (*Pause.*) Go over the pub.

ANNIE: Will you be OK? I mean, I'll back you up . . .

VIV: I'll be fine.

ANNIE: I'll wait for you over there.

VIV: I won't be long. (ANNIE *gets up. They look at one another. ANNIE goes. VIV goes to the door and shouts*:) Jane. (*Pause.*) Jane. I want to speak to you.

She sits. Pause. JANE comes back in. Pause.

If this is a taste of things to come, I think you'd better move out.

Pause.

JANE: If what is a taste of things to come?

VIV: This hostility.

Pause.

JANE: I'm sorry. I don't believe I'm hearing this. (*Pause.*) You're saying you want *me* to move out because *I'm* being hostile?

VIV: Yes.

JANE: That's absurd.

VIV: First of all, you bring your boyfriend here when you know that one of the house rules is no couples. Then you behave very hostile towards me, and then . . . This.

JANE: House rules? What the bloody hell are you talking about?

VIV: I don't want to live with a couple.

JANE: What were Rusty and Annie? What are you and Rusty now? And what's all this 'hostile' stuff?

VIV: I don't want to rationalise it.

JANE: You've got to. You can't just tell me to go.

VIV: I can and I am. (*Pause.*) Cleanliness.

JANE: What?

VIV: Cleanliness in the house. You don't do your bit.

JANE: I'm sorry, I do more than anybody else. I don't think you know what you're talking about.

VIV: You never clean the windows.

JANE: I what?!

VIV: That's right. You never clean the windows.

Pause.

JANE: You're mad. (*Pause.*) I mean it. You're insane. (*Pause. VIV just sips her drink.*) Come on, I want to discuss this.

VIV: Nothing to discuss.

JANE: There's everything to discuss.

VIV: I told you, I don't want to rationalise it.

JANE: But we're supposed to be rational people. Come on. Why do you want me to move out? (*Silence.*) Vivienne. (*Silence.*) Aren't you going to say anything?

VIV gets up and goes to the window and looks out. Then she goes to the oven and checks on the chicken. She washes out her glass and looks at the TV section in the paper. She makes this last a long time. Then she gets her things and goes to the door.

VIV: Goodbye. (*Pause. Then as if JANE is being unreasonable*:) Goodbye, Jane.

Silence. She goes. Pause. JANE sits on the sofa, close to tears.

Beat.

Fade.

Scene Two

Two and a half weeks later. It is about 7 p.m. TONE is sitting on the sofa. JANE is staring out the window. As the lights come up, TONE crushes an empty beer can, drops it in the bin and takes another from the fridge.

TONE: I'm gonna start thinkin' you've gone off me. (*Pause.*) If you don't fancy me any more, just say. (JANE *turns and looks at him then looks out the window again.*) You gonna stand at the window all night?

JANE: They're still in the pub.

Pause.

TONE: Marvellous. Thass made my night, that 'as. Fer fuck's sake . . .

JANE: I had to do without you when you were out playing cowboys and Indians.

TONE: That was different.

JANE: No, it wasn't. (*Pause.*) You've got plenty of sympathy for the people out there, but none for me. The only thing bothering you is you're not getting screwed as often as you'd like. Well I'm sorry. I don't feel like it. All right?

Pause.

TONE: Maybe we oughta . . .

JANE: What?

TONE: Knock it on the 'ead.

Pause.

JANE: You're just a bloody coward.

Pause.

TONE: Right. I'll go over the pub an' break their fuckin' arms, shall I? 'S that what you want? Or get 'em when they come through the door.

JANE: Is that all you know?

Beat.

TONE: Yeah! Thass all I know. Sorry.

JANE: Tone, I can't do it like that. I've got to know why. (*Pause.*) For over two weeks she hasn't spoken to me. None of them have. She avoids me. These people. My friends.

TONE: Middle class mind games.

JANE: The working class don't have a monopoly on misery, Tone!

TONE: Thass not what I meant! (*Pause.*) Look, this is fuckin' us up. It's fuckin' you up. Why don't you move out?

JANE: Where?

TONE: I dunno. (*Beat.*) My place? (*Long pause.*) Point taken.

JANE: We've only known each other six weeks.

TONE: Wouldn't 'ave to be permanent. (*Pause.*) Think about it.

JANE: I will. (*She walks around the room.*) She has that picture in her bedroom.

TONE: She don't know any better. She's not a fascist. She's just stupid.

JANE picks up an LP record and takes it out of its sleeve.

JANE: This is her favourite record. I want to scratch it.

Pause.

TONE: What is it?

JANE: Lou Reed.

TONE: Christ, scratch it. Call it a mercy killing.

JANE: Why don't I? (*Pause.*) Descending to her level.

TONE: Something like that. (*Pause.*) Oh, I'm very interested in that Rusty geezer. Considerin' 'oo 'is dad is. Very interested.

JANE: What d'you mean?

TONE: Thass all I'm sayin'.

Pause. JANE goes back to the window.

JANE: I just want to know why. It's not a lot to ask. Oh, God, they're coming back. Look at me. I dread it. I'm a wreck every time they come in. (TONE *goes to the door.*) Are you going upstairs?

TONE: Yeah. I'll just leave it a minute. (*He kisses her.*) Just act natural.

JANE: Some hope.

He goes. She looks around, momentary terror on her face, then picks up a book and starts to read. The door slams off. We hear talking and laughing. The door opens. VIV, BAZ, ANNIE and RUSTY come in. They're eating doner kebabs.

ANNIE: For the last time, I will not get anorexic just because I don't eat a rotten greasy kebab.

VIV: But you haven't eaten all day.

ANNIE: Because I don't want to.

RUSTY (*mock Jewish*): Eat, eat, you should eat. Your mama she say so.

BAZ *gets out a bottle of Demestica.*

BAZ: Here we are, then . . . a cheeky little vintage to remind you of that glorious Greek holiday. The chalky soil, the pungent grape, the gippy tum.

RUSTY (*reading the label*): Oh Baz, you have such style. A Nana Mouskouri evening. How quaint.

VIV (*to* ANNIE): Here, have some taramasalata at least.

ANNIE: OK. Makes a change from bloody pasta anyway.

RUSTY: Italy stories? Again? (*Pause.*) Anything on the box?

VIV: Have a look in the paper.

RUSTY: Where is it?

JANE *is half sitting on it. He sees it and gently tugs it from under her. She looks at him. He ignores her.*

VIV: Sure you don't want a bite?

ANNIE: I have to think of my figure.

RUSTY (*reading*): World in Action. Boring. News at Ten. Very boring. Ah. There's a film on later.

VIV: What is it?

RUSTY: Some American cop rubbish.

VIV: I got a job interview, by the way.

ANNIE: Terrific.

VIV: If I get it.

ANNIE: What's it for?

VIV: Nationwide. Researcher.

ANNIE: Christ. That's a bit high-powered.

VIV: No, not really. But it's an opening.

BAZ: Who knows, you might work your way up to Play School.

VIV: I wouldn't mind.

ANNIE: Any more news about Chelsea?

VIV: My folks won't budge. Anyway, I don't mind this place so much now. I think I've got used to it.

ANNIE: So . . .

VIV: Hmm. Yeah.

The door opens and TONE *comes in. Shocked silence at the table.*

TONE: Evenin' all. (*He sits.*)

Silence.

ANNIE: I heard a pleasant rumour that the band's kicked you out.

RUSTY: Oh yeah?

ANNIE: Yeah.

RUSTY: Shouldn't listen to rumours, darling. We're just not working at the moment.

ANNIE: Consideration for the audience?

RUSTY: Musical differences.

ANNIE: Ah. Like, they're musical, you're not.

RUSTY: Not at all. We're going in different directions, that's all. They want to stick with the synthesiser thing and I want to get into soul-funk. I want to use the Beggar and Co horn section, stuff like that. The others are just stuck in a rut, y'know? But, like, every band you hear today sounds the same, right? I just think we oughta move on. Anyway, I prefer the clothes.

ANNIE: I thought there must be a deeper reason.

TONE: Well, 'ello there.

Pause.

VIV: Can I have some more wine?

BAZ: Yeah. (*He pours them all some more.*)

ANNIE: Anyone see 'Holocaust' the other night?

RUSTY: Yeah.

ANNIE: What'd you think?

RUSTY: Bit one-sided.

BAZ *is embarrassed.*

TONE (*to* JANE): I see what you mean. (*Pause.*) Pathetic. Shall we go out? (TONE *and* JANE *get up.* TONE *turning to them at the door:*) We're over the pub if nobody wants to see us.

They go.

RUSTY: Bastard.

Pause.

ANNIE: Poor Viv. Isn't there anything you can do?

VIV: I've told her to go. She just hasn't moved.

BAZ: Well where d'you expect her to go? You can't just chuck her out on the streets. Give her time, for God's sake.

Beat.

VIV: Traitor.

Pause.

BAZ: Viv, in the five years I've known Jane, we've always got along fine. It's not easy treating someone you've known that well as if they're public enemy number one. Whatever happened, surely it's between the two of you. Why should I have to get involved?

VIV: You know I had a terrible row with her. You know what she thinks of me. What she said. (*Pause.*) She's hanging on here because she knows it makes me miserable. Doesn't that bother you?

ANNIE: Bloody well should.

VIV: She makes everything heavy, just being here. Just seeing her things in the bathroom makes me want to scream. I can't sleep at night with her on the other side of the wall. I hear her breathing. She doesn't sleep. She sits there knowing I'm awake. Knowing I'm awake because of her. And she's smiling. Thinks she's winning. And if I do sleep, I have a nightmare that she never goes away. Only she's not *in* the house any more, she *is* the house. She's everything, everywhere I look, I can't get away from her.

The door suddenly opens and TONE *comes in.*

TONE: Right . . .

RUSTY: What the fuck d'you want?!

Beat.

TONE: You'll do.

RUSTY (*very angry*): Well here I am. (*He gets up and advances on* TONE.) What's it to be, bully boy? Out on the pavement, or what? (*He starts jabbing* TONE *backwards.*) That what you're after? A good punch-up to satisfy your blood lust? Eh? You neanderthal ape. You fucking thick shithead. Come on, then. Or aren't you brave enough?

He's pushed TONE *against the wall. Suddenly* TONE *gives him a hard shove in the chest.*

TONE: Actually, pal, since you ask – (*He shoves him again.*) – the reason I came back over 'ere – (*He shoves him again;* RUSTY *falls into the chair.*) – is that I 'appen to be skint, an' you owe my bird a fiver. (*Pause.*) Now, if that money ain't forthcomin' pretty sharpish, bein' the neanderthal ape that I am, I'm gonna start pullin' your teeth out. Through the top o' your 'ead. Understand?

Pause.

RUSTY: I haven't got it.

TONE: Wrong.

RUSTY: I haven't.

Pause.

TONE: Then I 'ope your BUPA contributions are fully paid up.

BAZ *gets up and takes out his wallet and hands* TONE *a five pound note.*

You're a scholar an' a gentleman.

BAZ: Just fuck off, Tone.

TONE: My pleasure. (*Pause.*) 'Ave you seen what you done? 'Ave you looked at yourselves? 'Ave you? No. Can't be a lotta fun, lookin' at a room full o' shit. In fact, it ain't a lotta fun. So.

He goes.

BAZ: You silly bugger.

RUSTY: Get stuffed.

Pause.

VIV: Let's go out.

BAZ: Viv, you can't keep . . .

VIV: I can't keep what, Baz?!

BAZ: Nothing!

Pause.

ANNIE: Where d'you want to go?

VIV: Anywhere. Out.

ANNIE: Let's just drive. See where we end up.

VIV: Yeah.

RUSTY: I don't want to go driving.

ANNIE: So don't.

RUSTY: I *do* want to go out.

ANNIE: Oh, for Christ's sake, Rusty. Where d'you want to go?

RUSTY: I don't care! (*Pause. He gets up.*) I'm going. I'll see you later.

VIV (*as he gets to the door*): Rusty.

RUSTY: What? (*Pause.*) Look, Viv, I've just been pushed around on your account, and I don't like being pushed around. OK? I don't see why I should always take the stick. Always be the whipping boy.

ANNIE: Maybe if you kept your big mouth shut . . .

RUSTY: I'm talking to Viv. (*Pause.*) OK, V?

VIV: Is what OK?

RUSTY: I'm going out. Now.

VIV: But you haven't got any money.

RUSTY: I'll borrow some. Go home or something.

VIV: OK. (*Pause.*) That's OK.

Pause.

RUSTY: What's the catch?

VIV: Sorry?

RUSTY: How come you're letting me go?

VIV: I don't intend to run after you, if that's what you mean. Do whatever you like.

Pause.

RUSTY: And . . .

VIV: And nothing. (*Pause.*) Nobody loses any sleep over what you do. Don't flatter yourself. (*Pause.*) If you want to wait until we're ready, you can come with us. If you don't, off you go.

RUSTY: And don't come back.

VIV: Really, Rusty. What do you think I am? Vindictive? (*Pause.*) You're free to do what you want. Free as a bird. (*Pause.*)

RUSTY: I'll wait.

Pause.

VIV: Baz, you don't mind if Annie moves in when she goes, do you?

BAZ: Why should I mind? What's it got to do with me?

VIV: I want everybody to be happy.

BAZ: I'm happy. I'm ecstatic. Over the moon.

VIV: What's got into you?

BAZ: I just feel . . .

VIV: Cheer up. There's nothing to be miserable about.

BAZ: Two minutes ago . . .

VIV: Two minutes ago is two minutes ago. Forget it. Let's go out and enjoy ourselves.

BAZ: I can't.

VIV: Why not?

BAZ: I just can't.

Pause.

VIV: OK, let's go then.

RUSTY: Where?

VIV: Your house. Pick up some money. I'm broke.

BAZ: And you can get my fiver while you're there.

VIV: Right, well, let's go.

RUSTY: My father might be out . . .

ANNIE: Then we'll nick the family silver, OK?

VIV: See you, Baz.

BAZ: See you.

They go. Pause. BAZ *pours some more wine, puts on the TV and sits picking at the food.*

Fade.

Scene Three

Eleven-thirty that night. The TV set is flickering silently. BAZ *is seemingly asleep at the table, a half-empty bottle of scotch beside him. As the lights come up,*

*'Alison' by Elvis Costello is just finishing
on the record deck. Pause. The door opens
and JANE comes in. She takes the record
off and switches off the TV. BAZ raises
his head.*

BAZ: I was watching that. (*Pause.*) Only
joking. (*Pause.*) I must have nodded off.
(*He looks at the scotch bottle.*) Or put
meself to sleep. Drink? (*She shakes her
head. He takes a swig.*) I don't think this
bodes well for adult life. First sign of
trouble and we all dive head first into a
bottle. Still. Something to do, isn't it?
Somewhere to go. (*She goes to the kitchen
and pours coffee from the jug.*) Couldn't
do me one of those, could you? (*She
brings her cup and sits down.*) Ah. You
couldn't. I see. (*Pause.*) I was having a
dream there. I think. I mean, unless there
was a six-foot naked amazon in the room I
can only assume I was dreaming. (*Pause.*)
Spoke to my mum the other day. She
wanted to know why I haven't settled
down with a nice lass and got meself a
proper job. And, indeed, why haven't I?
All that fancy education, she said. Maybe
education stunted my growth. It's a
theory. (*Pause.*) Most of my old friends
are married, y'know. They send me
pictures. Those little instant polaroids
that make people look like inflatable
dolls. All my old friends seem to have
married inflatable dolls, in fact. If the
pictures are anything to go by. Handy for
the kids, eh? Last thing at night, you just
pull out their little belly buttons and the
air comes out. Then fold them up for the
night. Very handy. (*Pause. He takes a
swig.*) Whoosh. Say g'night, kids.
(*Pause.*) Actually, what have I got to
complain about? Nothing if you think
about it. Good job, nice car. Nice house.
(*Beat.*) Nice fucking house. Did you hear
that, eh? I sound like me mother.
(*Pause.*) Will you shut up and let me get a
word in edgeways. (*Pause.*) Most of my
old mates think I'm gay, I reckon. When I
go home for Christmas, I can hear them
thinking: yellow trousers? Only poofs
wear yellow trousers. (*Pause.*) I think I'm
too nice. I think I'm far too amenable.
Whatever that means. Sounds right. Sort
of me. Amenable. Sounds like a
government minister. We are amenable
to talks with the unions, but insist we
cannot budge an inch from our original
offer. Maybe I should have been a
politician. 'S easy enough. (*Pause.*) I'm
probably too nice to be a politician.
(*Pause.*) Too nice, too nice. Where does
it get you? (*Pause.*) You're nice. Not too
nice. Just nice. Which is nice. (*Pause.*)
Let me take you away from all this, I'll let
you take me away from all this if you like.
Never let it be said I'm not a feminist.
(*Pause.*) I think I'm the original little
man. How's that for self-awareness? (*He
takes a swig.*) Maybe I'm just going
through the male menopause thirty years
too early. (*Pause.*) I do enjoy these little
chats, y'know. A free and frank exchange
of views.

JANE: Why should I bother to talk to you?

BAZ: A question I've asked meself.

JANE: Well? Why should I?

BAZ: Dunno. (*Pause.*) Had a nice night?

JANE: Stop it, Baz.

BAZ: I've had a nice night. I've sat here all
on me own. Paradise.

JANE: You can't sit on your own forever.

BAZ: Aye. 'Appen. (*Pause.*) I've been
reading Henry James. Haven't read old
Henry since Oxford. (*Pause.*) Remember
when we were looking for a place? Before
Viv's folks bailed us out? It was gonna be
great, wasn't it? I had visions of sitting in a
book-lined room . . . dinner parties . . .
really civilized. (*Beat.*) Somewhere, up
there – (*He points.*) – was a malicious sod
pushing us around. Park Lane? Mayfair?
No chance. Go straight to jail. Do not
pass go. Do not collect two hundred
pounds. And here we bloody are.

JANE: We did it ourselves.

BAZ: No, I can't believe that. I mean,
surely we couldn't do this ourselves, not
even if we meant to. (*Pause.*) I'm sorry.
It's got out of hand. You're hurt. I'm
sorry about that.

JANE: Doesn't do me much good. I want to
know why.

BAZ: Ah.

JANE: Well?

Pause.

BAZ: You had a row with Viv.

JANE: I what? (*Pause.*) No.

Pause.

BAZ: Search me, then. That's what she says. Over and over. In case you didn't know, London is dotted with people who for no apparent reason see you as the new antichrist. Word has spread. (*Beat*.) And what can I do? It's embarrassing if I don't speak to you, and it's dangerous if I do. Least I've got a roof over my head, even if it does feel like it's caving in on me. (*Pause*.) And I've been a spineless jerk, haven't I?

Beat.

JANE: Yeah. You sat on the fence when you could have taken my side.

BAZ: Side?! (*Beat*.) It's mad. Taking sides. What *is* this?

JANE: I don't know, Baz, I didn't start it.

BAZ: Nobody did.

JANE: Viv did.

BAZ: All right, Viv did. (*Beat*.) OK? So. Any the wiser, are we?

Beat.

JANE: I thought you were my friend.

BAZ: Viv thinks I'm her friend.

JANE: You are.

BAZ: Fuck it. I'm nobody's friend. (*Pause*.) Least you've got Tone.

JANE: I don't know if I have any more. (*Beat*.) Wants me to go and live in his council flat in Battersea.

BAZ: Ethnic. (JANE *smiles*.) I like Tone.

JANE: So do I.

BAZ: Well . . . you saw him first.

They smile.

JANE: Baz, why does she hate me so much?

BAZ: I dunno. Honest. (*Beat*.) Property's not theft. It's something much worse. That much I do know.

RUSTY *enters. He takes a swig of Scotch*.

RUSTY: D'you know what they've done? D'you know what some bastard's gone and done? They've only gone and shopped me to the papers, haven't they? Paul bleeding Foot in the *Daily* bleeding *Mirror*. Bloody great article about *me*!

BAZ: Who has?

RUSTY: That's what I want to find out.

BAZ: What's it say?

RUSTY: Oh, nothing much. Just says how the son of the editor of the *Mirror*'s biggest rival lives off the dole at home with mummy and daddy, smoking dope and snorting coke.

BAZ: Well . . . It's true, you do . . .

RUSTY: I know it's true, Baz. What's that got to do with it? What I want to know is, why me? Eh? Who's idea of a joke *is* this?

BAZ: What's it matter?

RUSTY: Matters plenty, lamebrain. The publicity: great. I'll be famous. But I've just had two hours with my old man being roasted. And I mean burned. He's already famous y' see. He doesn't need it. He's talking life-support switch-off, man. No more money. I'm gonna be cut off without a penny. Savvy?

BAZ: You don't mean you'll have to get a job?

RUSTY: The sarcasm, Baz. Cut it. I've got big problems.

BAZ: You always got big problems.

Beat.

RUSTY: You, was it?

BAZ: What?

RUSTY: Been whispering in Comrade Foot's ear?

BAZ: Oh, go take a run. What d'you think I am?

RUSTY: A right little joker, that's what you are. Just your kind of stunt, this is. Drop Rusty in the shit. Give him a bad time. Well, joker, it's not funny. I'm not laughing.

BAZ: I don't know anything about it, prick.

RUSTY: Well, someone does.

Pause.

JANE: Why d'you think it was one of us? Bit obvious, isn't it?

RUSTY: Somewhere out there, there's a person with a grudge. A slimy little man who wants to get even. Christ, it's enough to make you paranoid. What next? Someone gonna take a shot at me or what? What?

BAZ: You're not John Lennon yet.

RUSTY: Fuck off, I mean it. I don't feel safe.

BAZ: Get a bodyguard.

RUSTY: Yeah. I might do that. (*The phone rings.*) I'm not here.

BAZ: If only. (*He picks up the phone.*) Yeah? (*Pause.*) Yeah. It's for me. Sorry. (*Back into the phone.*) Joey. If you're going to give me a hard time . . (*Pause.*) Don't do this to me, Joey. (*Pause.*) Listen . . . (*Pause. Joey's hung up.*) . . . You bastard. I don't believe it. Not again.

RUSTY: Do they know I'm here?

BAZ: Who?

RUSTY: Them.

BAZ: Fuck off, Rusty. Don't be a prat all your life, have a day off. (*He dials.*) Off the hook. (*Pause.*) Right.

He takes out his car keys and goes to the door.

JANE: Where you going?

BAZ: I'm gonna murder me a hippy.

He goes. JANE *stands, uncertain.*

RUSTY: Where are *you* going?

JANE: Bed.

RUSTY: What?

JANE: I'm tired.

RUSTY: I need someone to talk to.

JANE: Not me, surely.

RUSTY: You're the only person here.

JANE: I'm so sorry.

RUSTY: No, I mean . . .

JANE: I think it's rotten what's happened, but I still can't face the thought of having to talk to you. I'm sorry.

RUSTY: That's pretty sensitive of you.

JANE: No one ever thinks about *me*.

RUSTY: Please. I don't want to sit here on my own.

JANE: Neither did I. But I wasn't given any choice.

RUSTY: Please.

Pause. She sits.

JANE: I'm not very good at comforting the wounded.

RUSTY: 'S OK. (*Pause.*) I'm really freaked. I feel like a target.

JANE: You're not in any danger.

RUSTY: How do you know?

JANE: I'm using my head. (*Pause.*) Lots of people have stories printed about them. It's how your dad makes his living, isn't it?

RUSTY: He's a journalist, not a bastard.

JANE: You've obviously never read his paper.

RUSTY: Leave off my old man. He's just doing a job.

JANE: Where have I heard that before? (*Pause.*) Look, this is hopeless. I've got nothing to say to you. (*Pause.*) I don't feel very charitable. Things being the way they are.

RUSTY: What things?

JANE: You mean you hadn't noticed?

RUSTY: Oh, all that. It's nothing.

JANE (*standing*): Honestly, Rusty, if you're going to stand there and shrug off my problems as if they don't exist and expect me to take yours seriously, I might as well go to bed.

RUSTY: *We* might as well go to bed.

Beat.

JANE: I'm going to pretend I didn't hear that.

RUSTY: Why? Sex is a good therapy.

JANE: God, you're offensive.

RUSTY: You're very attractive. I fancy you, right? What's offensive about that? It's a compliment.

JANE: Go to hell.

RUSTY: You really are hung up, aren't you? Just where'd you get this idea that you're so bloody important?

Beat.

JANE: I hope there is a man out there with a gun, waiting to shoot you. You deserve it.

Pause.

RUSTY: Viv's right, isn't she? You are a nasty piece of work. Very sweet on the outside, but it's a real snake pit inside there, isn't it? (*Pause.*) Pity we couldn't make it. I bet you're really good. Really rough.

JANE: Curl up and die.

She starts to go.

RUSTY: You should lose some of those hang-ups, y'know. There's nothing worse than a tight-assed chick. (*She turns and stares at him.*) What you gonna do? Set your gorilla on me? Wheel out the working class hero to do his macho bit? (*Pause.*) You should ditch him, y'know. So fucking straight. Thinks Victoria's still on the fucking throne, right? God, how boring. We're classless now. Someone should tell him. Put him out of his misery. And you. Get into some personal liberation. Get into your own head. Might loosen you up a bit.

Pause.

JANE: That's why you never make any sense. You got 'into your own head'. And it's so empty in there, you probably got lost. Round and round in circles. Looking at yourself. A pointless exercise for a pointless person. (*Beat.*) You're not classless. You're dead.

She goes.

RUSTY: I bet you're frigid, anyway!

Pause. He sits and thinks then goes to the window and looks out. He turns out most of the lights then looks out the window again. He thinks, goes to the phone and dials.

Hi. Carolyn? It's Rusty. (*Pause.*) Terrible. I've had a bit of a shock. (*Pause.*) I was wondering if I could come round. (*Pause.*) I know it's late, but I really need someone to talk to. (*Pause.*) I'll tell you about it when I come round. I'm really freaked. (*Pause.*) I'll get a cab. (*Pause.*) You're an angel. I'll be there in about twenty minutes. (*Pause.*) You got any booze? (*Pause.*) OK. I'll see you. Bye.

He puts the phone down, looks round the room, picks up the scotch from the table and goes, turning the lights out.

Scene Four

About two weeks later. Late afternoon. BAZ is in the kitchen cleaning the oven and worktops. RUSTY comes on. He's bare-chested, listening to BAZ's Walkman and has been snorting cocaine. He stands centre stage.

BAZ: That's ninety-nine quid's worth of advanced Nip technology you've got on there. Mind how you go.

RUSTY *just stares at him, singing 'Goes on, and the beat goes on . . .' BAZ goes over to him and talks at him while he sings.*

Gonna be difficult, are you. Gonna fuck it all up? Poke your tongue out at teacher? Fag behind the bike sheds? That the game, is it?

RUSTY: I see your lips moving. I don't hear any words.

BAZ: What are Viv's folks supposed to make of you, eh? Man of mystery? (RUSTY *takes the headphones off.*) Why don't you do something to help?

RUSTY: I don't *dig* graves, man, I dance on them.

He puts the headphones back on and sings along. BAZ shrugs as VIV comes in carrying a pile of papers. BAZ sits.

VIV: Rusty . . . (RUSTY *turns and goes. She stares at BAZ.*) What are you doing?

BAZ: I'm having a breather.

VIV: Don't take all day. There's still the floor to do. (*Pause.*) And don't sulk.

Pause. JANE enters, goes to the record and takes out two or three. VIV stares. JANE goes with her record. Pause. VIV looks through the records.

BAZ: They were hers.

VIV: How do you know? (*She goes on checking, then sits again.*)

BAZ: Well?

VIV: If it's not screwed down, she'll try to take it. (*Pause.*) My shampoo was gone this morning. (*Pause.*) You'll never get finished at this rate. And I want this place looking spotless. (BAZ *gets up and goes back to the kitchen.*) Make sure you're changed before they arrive.

BAZ: I've washed behind my ears.

VIV: For a change. (*She looks out the window.*) She'd better be gone when they get here.

BAZ: I don't s'pose she's exactly dying to meet your folks.

VIV: She'll do anything to start a scene. (*Pause.*) And where the hell is Annie? She should have been back ages ago. (*Pause.*) Shit. I'll never get these bills sorted out in time.

BAZ: Stop fussing.

VIV: Everything's got to be right. Dad wants to see all the bills. And he wants to see this place looking good. If anything's not right, he'll go through the roof.

BAZ: I'm sure he can afford a new one. (*Pause.*) Just a joke.

VIV: Save the jokes for later.

BAZ: Oh, I will be allowed a joke then, will I?

VIV: When they've had a look round.

BAZ: But not before.

VIV: Just hurry up, will you? (BAZ *starts mopping the kitchen floor. A door slams offstage.*) About time (ANNIE *comes in carrying Sainsbury's carrier bags.*) D'you get everything? (RUSTY *enters with coke and a mirror.*)

ANNIE: Just about. Took hours getting through the checkout. Bloody supermarkets are hell. Grubby housewives shoving you all over the place.

RUSTY *goes to the kitchen.*

BAZ: Don't get on my wet floor!

RUSTY (*looking at the floor*): Walking on water again. Aren't I a one?

BAZ: You're a fucking idiot.

VIV: Rusty, get out of the way, and don't make a mess anywhere. And, Baz, don't keep swearing when they get here.

RUSTY (*laughing*): Fucking hell . . .

VIV: The next time you say that I'll brain you, I mean it. (*To* BAZ:) You'll have to do the floor again in a minute.

VIV *and* ANNIE *sort the shopping out, putting it in the fridge and cupboards.*

BAZ: Great. (*He sits down.*)

VIV: Don't waste time. You might as well get changed.

He gets up and goes. JANE *enters and looks round the room to see if she's forgotten anything. She notices a book, picks it up and goes.*

If she's not gone . . .

ANNIE: How long have we got?

VIV: Not long. They'll have left Tim and Sheila's by now.

ANNIE: Everything OK?

VIV: I think so. D'you get the cassette?

ANNIE: Yeah. Had to go over to Clapham for it. You ever tried buying Vivaldi in Brixton?

RUSTY: Vivaldi. (*He snorts.*)

VIV: My mum happens to like it. Nothing wrong with that.

RUSTY: Beats Valium, I s'pose

Pause.

ANNIE: Can we have a drink?

VIV: If you like. You can be in charge of the drinks, Rusty. Keep them topped up. Sherry for mum, scotch for dad, with lots of ice.

RUSTY: In the sherry?

VIV: In the scotch.

ANNIE: Come on then, Rusty. Chop chop.

RUSTY: Feel like a bloody butler.

VIV: No. You feel like a butler. No bloody. Got it.

RUSTY: Feel . . . like . . . a butler. Got it.

VIV: Good. So act like one. Get me a scotch.

ANNIE: And me.

He does. He's gradually becoming more and more annoyed and tense.

What about you?

RUSTY: I think I'll give it a miss.

ANNIE: What's the matter? Got the clap again?

He gives a sheepish grin and sits down.

VIV (*going back to the bills*): What d'you know about sport, Rusty?

He laughs.

Baz'll have to cover that. Dad's crazy about football. Has videos of all the big games sent out to him.

RUSTY: I'll be arts correspondent, shall I?

VIV: They're not interested in the arts.

RUSTY: Then I'll just keep my big mouth shut.

ANNIE: Where are we going to eat?

VIV: I booked a table at San Lorenzo's.

ANNIE: That'll cost.

VIV: Dad's paying.

ANNIE: I like him already.

VIV: You can show off your Italian.

ANNIE: God I only know a few words.

RUSTY: Like 'yes, please.'

Pause.

ANNIE (*to* VIV): Isn't it funny how people can be so jealous. I mean to say, I only got myself a fabulous job in Italy, terrific money, sun, and my weight in coke. Nothing special, really.

BAZ *comes back in wearing a different shirt and tying a tie.*

Get you.

BAZ: I thought if I made a good impression they might adopt me. (*He pours a drink.*) Rusty?

RUSTY: No.

BAZ: You ill or something?

VIV: Floor's free if you want to mop it.

BAZ: Bloody hell.

RUSTY (*sharp intake of breath*): Hell. No bloody.

BAZ: Eh?

RUSTY: No swearing. By order.

VIV: That's right. By order. My order.

RUSTY: Just telling him.

VIV: You were getting at me. Don't.

RUSTY: What are we supposed to do? Suspend all normal behaviour?

VIV: Precisely.

RUSTY: You frightened of them, or what?

VIV: No. They happen to be my parents and they happen to own the house. And that entitles them to a little consideration. Besides, I think that's pretty rich coming from someone who cringed and crawled not to be thrown out of home. Don't you?

Pause.

RUSTY: Shit. I'm off. (*He stands.*)

VIV: When you go through that door, you don't come back. Ever. (*He sits.*) Good boy.

BAZ: What do we call them?

VIV: What?

BAZ: Your folks. Can't very well call them mum and dad, can we?

VIV: 'Course not. (*Beat.*) Call them by their first names. That'll be OK.

BAZ: Right. (*Beat.*) What are their first names?

VIV: Oh. Bill and Doreen. (RUSTY *suppresses a hysterical laugh.*) What?

RUSTY (*barely able to get the words out*): Nothing . . .

VIV: What's so funny, Rusty?

RUSTY: I don't know . . .

She goes over to him.

VIV: What the bloody hell are you laughing at?!

RUSTY (*exploding with laughter*): BILL AND DOREEN! SOUNDS LIKE THEY RUN A WHELK STALL!

VIV *takes his coke and flushes it down the sink.*

VIV: Now, get out.

RUSTY: Why?

VIV: I won't have you sitting here making cheap comments. I've had enough of people sniping at me. And I don't have to take it from a parasite like you.

BAZ: Who'd like another drink?

RUSTY: Parasite?

VIV: Yeah. Sponging little parasite.

RUSTY: Takes one to know one, lovey. Least I own up to it.

VIV: Could hardly do anything else, could you?

RUSTY: Why should I want to? I'm proud of it. Best looking maggot in the heap, me.

ANNIE: Maggot's about right.

RUSTY: Ah. Talking of parasites. (*Beat.*) Little miss glam jet-set here. The globe-trotting mdel. Well . . . from what Dennis tells me, and he tells me plenty, your oh-so-fabulous Italian job was no more than a series of beaver shots, darling. And some very steamy group shots, darling. In short, porn-og-raphy, darling.

Pause.

ANNIE: Liar.

RUSTY (*picks up the phone*): Shall we ring him? Ask him? (*Pause.*) No? (*He puts the phone down.*) We had quite a laugh about it. Me and Dennis . . . and Alison and Raif and Carolyn . . .

VIV: Leave her alone!

RUSTY: Stop giving me fucking orders!

BAZ: Someone tell me why this is going on now.

RUSTY: No time like the present. Right? (*He sits back.*) Where are they, then, Viv? I'm positively wetting myself with anticipation at the thought of meeting Bill and Noreen. Noreen, was it? Or Doreen? Remind me.

BAZ: Pretty cheap, making fun of peoples' names, isn't it?

RUSTY: Don't try to be sincere, Baz. It turns my stomach. (*He takes out more coke and makes up a line on the mirror.*)

VIV: My dad'll throw you out when he gets here.

RUSTY: I can't wait. Fancy a line? (*Pause.*) I should have thought it was very much your style. Everything in lines. Dead straight. Shoulders back. Arms folded. (*He goes to BAZ.*) Come on, Baz. This is worth a team point. This is important. Sit up straight. Come on. (BAZ *slouches.*) Viv won't like it, Baz. Viv likes things her way. Row after row of adoring fans all saying 'Yes, Viv. No, Viv. Lick your arse, Viv'. Come on, Baz, Annie. Viv wants you to lick her arse. This is important. Come on. (*He goes down on his knees and grabs at* VIV.) I thought Jane was the only one who wouldn't do it. It's OK, Viv, I'll do it. I'll lick your arse, Viv. (*She pulls away.*) Come on. THIS IS IMPORTANT!

Pause.

VIV: You're a mess, Rusty.

RUSTY (*worn out*): So hoover me up into your little dirt bag. I'm a stain. Rub me out.

ANNIE: You're a bastard.

RUSTY: YES! We all are. So let's admit it and have a good time. Don't stand there peeping through your net curtains at me. Say something, anything. (*Pause.*) Nothing? Not even a little twitch?

VIV *hands him a piece of paper.*

What's this?

VIV: Your share of the bills since you've been living here.

RUSTY (*laughing*): I'll send you a cheque.

VIV: Now run along.

RUSTY: What, playtime over already?

VIV: That's right. (*He goes over to her, close.*)

RUSTY: You're getting grey hairs. They suit you. (*Pause.*) It's OK. I've found someone else to move in with. (*Pause.*) I *was* going to tell you. Honest.

VIV: You have.

RUSTY: Yeah.

VIV: What's she like?

RUSTY: A bastard. Claws bared. The real thing. I'm sure we'll be very happy together.

VIV: I'm sure.

Pause.

BAZ: Time's getting on.

Pause.

RUSTY: I thought it was important.

He smiles. Pause. He starts to go.

Oh . . . about the drink . . . why I'm not . . . You were right first time, Annie. I've got the clap. (*Beat.*) Which means that you've got the clap, and Viv's got the clap. (*Beat.*) Lucky ol' Baz does it again.

BAZ: Oh no, he doesn't. (*He and* ANNIE *look at each other.*)

RUSTY: Well, really. There's hope for you all yet. (*Pause.*) OK. I'll see you guys around. No hard feelings, right? Ciao.

He goes.

ANNIE: That's not true about Italy . . . I did a couple of shots . . . semi-nude . . . but . . .

VIV: I didn't know you two had . . . (*Pause.*) You should have told me.

BAZ: Maybe we should have asked permission.

VIV: I just like to know.

Pause.

ANNIE: Sod Rusty. I hate that clinic. Sordid bloody place.

BAZ: You're obviously old hands at this.

ANNIE: Could say that.

BAZ: Yeah. Well, it's my first time.

ANNIE: It's nothing to worry about. probably NSU. Rusty's got it more or less permanent. You take anti-biotics for a week then it's gone. Think of it as being promoted to the first division. You're a big boy now.

Pause.

VIV: You didn't finish the floor, Baz.

BAZ: Oh, Christ . . .

VIV: It's not the end of the world. Forget it. Act as if nothing's happened.

BAZ: How can I? We're gonna be sat here, being nice to your folks, knowing we've all got bloody VD.

VIV: Just don't think about it.

BAZ: I'm gonna feel a bloody fool.

VIV: That's all right.

Pause.

BAZ (*stops and thinks*): The bastard's got my Walkman.

Long pause.

VIV: The floor.

Pause. He starts mopping. JANE *and* TONE *enter.*

JANE: All my stuff's out. I'm going.

VIV *hands her a piece of paper.*

VIV: Here.

JANE *and* TONE *read it. He laughs.*

TONE: You must be joking.

JANE: I've no intention of paying you a penny.

ANNIE: Pound of flesh?

JANE: I think I'm entitled to hurt you back, don't you?

TONE (*screwing the paper into a ball and throwing it into the bin*): What she's sayng is: you can whistle for it. You know how to whistle, don't you? Just put your lips together an' blow.

Pause.

JANE: Goodbye. (*She starts to go.*)

TONE *goes to the kitchen and points at the floor.*

You missed a bit.

TONE *and* JANE *go.*

ANNIE: Sue her. Take her to court.

BAZ: Don't be daft.

ANNIE: Can't let her get away with that.

BAZ: She's gone. That's all there is to it.

VIV *puts the bills into neat piles and looks around the room.*

VIV: Right. I think everything's ready. Put the mop away, Baz. (*He does.*) You can move in whenever you want.

ANNIE: Yeah.

VIV: You'll probably want to decorate, won't you?

ANNIE: Could do.

VIV: Me and Baz'll help, won't we, Baz? We could maybe do the whole house. Be good fun. Doing it together. (*Pause. She straightens* BAZ's *tie.*) Now we can all just settle down, thank God. No more hassles. We're free. (*She gives* BAZ *the Vivaldi tape,* The Four Seasons, *and he puts it on. The doorbell rings.*) That's them. (*Pause.*) OK. Big smiles, everyone.

The music starts.

End